How to have a Luxury Trip to Switzerland on a Budget.

The first glimpse of the Swiss mountains is not a mere sight; it's a visceral experience, a breathtaking revelation that transcends the visual and etches itself onto the canvas of your memory.

Welcome to your guide to a Luxury Trip to Switzerland on a budget!

This travel guide is your step-by-step manual for unlocking luxury hotels, enjoying the best culinary offerings and once-in-a-lifetime luxury experiences in Switzerland at a fraction of the usual cost.

Everyone's budget is different, but luxury is typically defined by first or business class seats on the airplane, five-star hotels, chauffeurs, exclusive experiences, and delectable fine dining. Yes, all of these can be enjoyed on a budget.

Finding luxury deals in Switzerland simply requires a bit of research and planning, which this book has done for you. We have packed this book with local insider tips and knowledge to save you tens of thousands.

If the mere mention of the word luxury has you thinking things like "Money doesn't grow on trees," "I don't need anything fancy," "I don't deserve nice things," or "People who take luxury trips are shallow and materialistic/environmentally harmful/lack empathy, etc.," then stop. While we all know travel increases our happiness, research on the effects of luxury travel has proven even better results:

Reduced stress: A study published in the Journal of Travel Research found that individuals who visited luxury hotels reported feeling less stressed than those who in standard hotels.[1]

Increased happiness: A study conducted by the International Journal of Tourism Research found that luxury travel experiences lead to an increase in happiness and overall life satisfaction.[2] Researchers also found that luxury travel experiences can improve individuals' mental health by providing a sense of escape from daily stressors and enhancing feelings of relaxation and rejuvenation.

Enhanced creativity: Researchers found engaging in luxury travel experiences can stimulate creativity and lead to more innovative thinking.[3]

While all of this makes perfect sense; it feels much nicer to stay in a hotel room that's cleaned daily than in an Airbnb where you're cleaning up after yourself. What you might not know is that you can have all of that increased happiness and well-being without

---

[1] Wöber, K. W., & Fuchs, M. (2016). The effects of hotel attributes on perceived value and satisfaction. Journal of Travel Research, 55(3), 306-318.

[2] Ladhari, R., Souiden, N., & Dufour, B. (2017). Luxury hotel customers' satisfaction and loyalty: An empirical study. International Journal of Hospitality Management, 63, 1-10.

[3] Kim, S., Kim, S. Y., & Lee, H. R. (2019). Luxury travel, inspiration, and creativity: A qualitative investigation. Tourism Management, 71, 354-366.

emptying your bank account. Does it sound too good to be true? This book will prove it isn't!

The Magical Power of Bargains

Have you ever felt the rush of getting a bargain? And then found good fortune just keeps following you?

Let me give you an example. In 2009, I graduated into the worst global recession for generations. One unemployed day, I saw a suit I knew I could get a job in. The suit was £250. Money I didn't have. Imagine my shock when the next day I saw the exact same suit (in my size) in the window of a second-hand shop (thrift store) for £18! I bought the suit and after three months of interviewing, without a single call back, within a week of owning that £18 suit, I was hired on a salary far above my expectations. That's the powerful psychological effect of getting an incredible deal. It builds a sense of excitement and happiness that literally creates miracles.

Imagine standing atop the Swiss Alps, surrounded by pristine snow-capped peaks, and knowing that your journey was not only a feast for the senses but also a wise investment in your pocket. The detailed insights, hacks, and insider tips seamlessly woven into the fabric of this guide ensure that your adventure is luxurious and budget-friendly.

I have no doubt that the incredible vistas and mountains of Switzerland will uplift and inspire you but when you add the bargains from this book to your vacation, not only will you save a ton of money; you are guaranteed to enjoy a truly magical trip to Switzerland.

Who this book is for and why anyone can enjoy luxury travel on a budget

Did you know you can fly on a private jet for $500? Yes, a fully private jet. Complete with flutes of champagne and reclinable creamy leather seats. Your average billionaire spends $20,000 on the exact same flight. You can get it for $500 when you book private jet empty leg flights.This is just one of thousands of ways you can travel luxuriously on a budget. You see there is a big difference between being cheap and frugal.

When our brain hears the word "budget" it hears deprivation, suffering, agony, even depression. But budget travel need not be synonymous with hostels and pack lunches. You can enjoy an incredible and luxurious trip to Switzerland on a budget, just like you can enjoy a private jet flight for 10% of the normal cost when you know how.

Over 20 years of travel has taught me I could have a 20 cent experience that will stir my soul more than a $100 one. Of course, sometimes the reverse is true, my point is, spending money on travel is the best investment you can make but it doesn't have to be at levels set by hotels and attractions with massive ad spends and influencers who are paid small fortunes to get you to buy into something you could have for a fraction of the cost.

This book is for those who love bargains and want to have the cold hard budget busting facts to hand (which is why we've included so many one page charts, which you can use as a quick reference), but otherwise, the book provides plenty of tips to help you shape your own Switzerland experience.

We have designed these travel guides to give you a unique planning tool to experience an unforgettable trip without spending the ascribed tourist budget.

This guide focuses on Switzerland's unbelievable bargains. Of course, there is little value in traveling to Switzerland and not experiencing everything it has to offer. Where possible, we've included super cheap workarounds or listed the experience in the Loved but Costly section.

When it comes to luxury budget travel, it's all about what you know. You can have all the feels without most of the bills. A few days spent planning can save you thousands. Luckily, we've done the planning for you, so you can distill the information in minutes not days, leaving you to focus on what matters: immersing yourself in the sights, sounds and smells of Switzerland, meeting awesome new people and feeling relaxed and happy.

This book reads like a good friend has travelled the length and breadth of Switzerland and brought you back incredible insider tips.

So, grab a cup of tea or coffee, put your feet up and relax; you're about to enter the world of enjoying Switzerland on the Super Cheap. Oh, and don't forget a biscuit. You need energy to plan a trip of a lifetime on a budget.

Discover Switzerland

Switzerland, a country where mountains command a staggering 70% of its landscape, is a captivating blend of natural wonders and cultural riches. From the majestic panoramas of Interlaken to the alpine charm of Zermatt, Switzerland has beckoned travelers for centuries, spawning a myriad of resorts, ranging from the opulence of St. Moritz to the backpacker-friendly Jungfrau Region.

Beyond the Alps, the country reveals a tapestry of culture and history in towns like Gruyeres and Montreux. Major cities such as Zurich and Geneva pulsate with vibrant nightlife, while the warmth of Italian influence bathes Bellinzona and Lugano in sunshine. Seeking solitude? Retreat to the quaint villages of Grindelwald or Lauterbrunnen, where Switzerland unfolds like pages from a timeless tale.

Switzerland, with one of the world's highest standards of living, seamlessly blends German, French, and Italian cultures, offering a unique 'three-in-one' experience. While expenses may test even the most generous budget, there are many hacks and the return on investment is unparalleled – impeccable infrastructure, breathtaking landscapes, and memories etched for a lifetime.

As you traverse cobbled streets of medieval towns and explore the pulsating energy of modern cities, Switzerland unfolds as a land where time seems to stand still amidst the breathtaking beauty of the Swiss Alps and the rich tapestry of its historical and cultural wonders. Nestled in the heart of Europe, Switzerland is a landlocked symphony of landscapes, from pristine lakes to iconic mountain peaks, charming villages, and vibrant cities.

Switzerland's cities are living stories, where Michelin-starred restaurants sit alongside historic landmarks, and local markets exude a vibrant, cultural pulse.

Known for its policy of neutrality, Switzerland has not been involved in any military conflict since 1815, relying on a well-trained militia and hosting the founding of the International Committee of the Red Cross in 1863. Orson Welles famously said "In Switzerland, they had brotherly love, they had 500 years of democracy and peace – and what did that produce? The cuckoo clock." Well Orson, at least its beautifully precise!

Embark on a journey where crisp mountain air becomes your constant companion, alpine meadows transform into your secluded sanctuary, and the gentle echoes of cowbells serenade both the luxury traveler and the savvy explorer on a budget. Switzerland beckons, offering an invitation to embrace a travel experience where luxury isn't a privilege solely for the elite—it's a promise accessible to every wanderer.

What you need to know before you visit Switzerland

- **Currency:** Switzerland uses the Swiss Franc (CHF), and cash is widely accepted. Credit cards are also commonly used, but it's advisable to carry some cash, especially in smaller towns.
- **Language Diversity:** Switzerland has four official languages – German, French, Italian, and Romansh. The language spoken depends on the region you are in, so it's helpful to know some basic phrases in each. They are included at the end of the guide.
- **Public Transportation:** The Swiss public transportation system is renowned for its efficiency. Trains, buses, and boats connect even the most remote areas. Consider getting a Swiss Travel Pass for unlimited travel on public transportation and access to over 500 museums. Prices start at 232 CHF.
- **Punctuality:** Swiss people are known for their punctuality. Whether it's public transportation, meetings, or social gatherings, being on time is highly valued.
- **Tipping Culture:** Service charges are usually included in bills, but it's customary to round up the amount or leave a small tip in restaurants. Tipping in cafes and for services like taxis is also common.
- **Weather Variability:** Switzerland's weather can change quickly, especially in mountainous regions. Pack layers, including a waterproof jacket, regardless of the season. It's advisable to check the weather forecast before planning outdoor activities.
- **Cultural Respect:** Swiss culture places importance on politeness and respect. Greetings are typically a handshake, and it's customary to say "hello" and "goodbye" when entering or leaving a room.
- **Hiking Essentials:** If you plan on exploring the Swiss Alps, ensure you have suitable hiking gear, including sturdy shoes, a map, and plenty of water. Weather conditions in mountainous areas can be unpredictable.
- **Altitude Sickness:** Gradual acclimatization to high altitudes is key to preventing altitude sickness. Ensure you stay hydrated and limit alcohol intake during your stay in elevated areas.
- **Tick-borne Diseases:** Switzerland, like many other regions with forests and grassy areas, does have a tick population, and tick-borne diseases are a concern. Protect yourself from tick-borne diseases by wearing long sleeves and pants in wooded or grassy areas, using insect repellent containing DEET, and regularly checking for ticks.
- **Water Quality:** Switzerland has strict regulations and standards for water quality, and the tap water is subject to regular testing to ensure it meets these standards. Tap water in Switzerland is safe to drink, so there's no need to buy bottled water. Bring a reusable water bottle to stay hydrated, especially during outdoor activities.
- **Shopping Hours:** Shops in Switzerland often close early, with many closing around 6 or 7 pm on weekdays and even earlier on Saturdays. Plan your shopping accordingly, and be aware that many stores are closed on Sundays.
- **Square Flag:** Switzerland is the only sovereign state with a square flag. The white cross on a red background is an iconic symbol of the country.

- **Direct Democracy:** Switzerland practices a form of direct democracy, allowing citizens to participate in decision-making through referendums. This system empowers the population to have a direct impact on legislation.
- **Champion of Innovation:** Despite its small size, Switzerland consistently ranks high in global innovation indices. The country invests heavily in research and development, fostering a culture of innovation and technology advancement.
- **Swiss banking secrecy** has been significantly reduced in recent years due to international pressure and regulatory changes. Swiss banks now adhere to global standards on financial transparency.

Some of Switzerland's Best Bargains

Discount Passes

Super organised Switzerland offers several incredible discount passes for travelers. Used the right way, you can save thousands with the discount passes but it will depend on your travel plans and preferences. Here's a chart to help you make sense of them.

Membership	Description	Cost	Benefits	Potential Savings	Website
Swiss Travel Pass	Unlimited travel on public transportation (trains, buses, boats) and free entry to many museums.	Varies (e.g., 3-day pass for CHF 232)	Free transportation, free museum entry, discounts on mountain excursions.	Significant savings on transportation and museum fees.	Swiss Travel Pass
Swiss Half Fare Card	Allows you to travel by train, bus, and boat and most mountain railways at half price.	CHF 60 for one month	50% off on various modes of transportation, including mountain railways.	Half-price transportation, potential savings on mountain excursions.	Swiss Half Fare Card
Museum Pass	Grants access to many museums across Switzerland for a specified period.	Museum Pass from CHF 32	Free entry to numerous museums and cultural attractions.	Depending on the number of museums visited, significant savings.	Swiss Museums
Youth Hostel Membership	Provides discounts on accommodations at Swiss Youth Hostels.	CHF 33 per year	Reduced rates on stays at Youth Hostels.	Savings on accommodation costs for budget-conscious travelers.	Swiss Youth Hostels
ZurichCARD	Offers unlimited 2nd class travel by tram, bus, train, boat, cableway, and funicular in the city of Zurich.	CHF 27 for 24 hours	Free public transportation, free entry to participating museums, and discounts at various attractions.	Savings on transportation and entry fees in Zurich.	ZurichCARD
Geneva Pass	- Free public transport	Jet d'Eau, St. Pierre Cathedral, and the Red Cross Museum	$25/day	Geneva Pass	- Free public transport
Basel Card	- Free public transport		Basel Minster, Rhine River Cruise, and Kunstmuseum Basel	$20/day	
Lucerne Card	- Free public transport		Lion Monument, Mount Pilatus, and Lake Lucerne Cruise	$30/day	

Family passes in Switzerland

If you are travelling as a family, you can also cut costs considerably with passes. Here's a simplified chart comparing some family passes in Switzerland:

Family Pass	Duration	Costs	Benefits
Swiss Travel Pass Family	3, 4, 8, or 15 days	Kids 6 - 16 travel free with parents with a Swiss travel pass.	Unlimited travel on trains, buses, and boats. Free admission to many museums. Children under 16 travel free with a family pass holder.
Half Fare Card for Families	1 month	CHF 30 (for 1 adult and 1 child) + CHF 15 for each additional child	50% discount on most trains, buses, and boats. Children under 6 travel for free.
Junior Card	1 year	CHF 30	Children aged 6 to 16 travel for free on most public transportation when accompanied by at least one parent with a valid ticket.

Stay in a Castle

You don't need a royal budget to stay in a Swiss castle. The Swiss Castle Association estimates that there are around 5,000 castles, fortresses, and towers in Switzerland.

During the medieval period, Switzerland was not a unified nation but a collection of independent territories, principalities, and regions. Local rulers, such as counts and dukes, built castles as both symbols of their authority and as defensive structures to protect their territories. These structures range from well-preserved castles with historical significance to more modest structures that may have served as defensive outposts in the past. Here are some castles you can stay in for less than 40 CHF a night!

- **Avenches Castle Youth Hostel:** Located in Avenches, this youth hostel is set in a historic castle and offers budget-friendly accommodation.
- **Mariastein Castle Youth Hostel:** Situated near Basel, this youth hostel is housed in the Mariastein Castle and provides a unique setting for travelers on a budget.
- **Schloss Wartegg:** Located near Lake Constance, Schloss Wartegg is a castle hotel that combines historic charm with modern amenities. While it may not be the cheapest, it offers a unique experience.

- **Schloss Laufen am Rheinfall:** This castle is situated near the famous Rhine Falls. It has a youth hostel within its premises, providing budget accommodation options.

Train Travel

As the train glides through picturesque valleys and ascends majestic mountains and the crisp alpine air fills your lungs the panoramic views of snow-capped peaks, emerald lakes, and charming villages will create an inedible memory. Best of all, Switzerland offers scenic train journeys that can be enjoyed both luxuriously and on a budget.

Glacier Express:

Indulge in elegance aboard the Glacier Express Excellence Class, featuring panoramic windows and gourmet meals for a truly lavish journey.

Bernina Express:

Elevate your travel experience with first-class tickets on the Bernina Express, offering added comfort and a premium perspective on picturesque landscapes. Consider the panoramic car with large windows for an immersive journey.

GoldenPass Line:

Enjoy VIP treatment on the GoldenPass Classic with first-class seats, boasting a glass roof and personalized service for an exclusive and refined travel experience.

Gotthard Panorama Express:

Luxuriate in first-class comfort on the Gotthard Panorama Express, where panoramic windows offer breathtaking views. Consider adding a cruise on Lake Lucerne for an extra layer of luxury.

Zürich to Interlaken Express:

Opt for first-class accommodations on the Zürich to Interlaken Express for a more comfortable ride with superior amenities.

Voralpen Express:

Indulge in extra comfort and amenities with first-class tickets on the Voralpen Express, ensuring a premium travel experience where opulence and tranquility define every moment.

These luxurious train adventures promise not just a visual feast but a journey where every detail is adorned with sophistication and comfort, making your exploration through the scenic beauty of Switzerland truly extraordinary.

Upgrading to first class on Swiss trains is affordable with these tips:

- **Off-Peak Travel:** Traveling during off-peak hours or on less busy days might increase your chances of finding discounted first-class tickets.
- **Book in Advance:** Many train operators offer 80% discounts for early bookings.
- **Swiss Travel Pass:** Consider purchasing a Swiss Travel Pass for unlimited travel on trains, buses, and boats, as well as free entry to many museums

Here's a simplified table comparing different Swiss Rail Passes, their costs, benefits, and potential savings. Keep in mind that prices and details may change, so it's essential to check the official Swiss Travel System website for the most up-to-date information.

Swiss Rail Pass	Cost (in CHF)	Validity	Benefits	Potential Savings*
Swiss Travel Pass	3 days: 232	3, 4, 8, or 15 days	Unlimited travel on the Swiss Travel System network, free or discounted entry to museums, free boat trips, and more.	High, especially if you plan to travel extensively.
Swiss Half Fare Card	120	1 month	Allows you to travel by train, bus, and boat and most mountain railways at half price.	Significant savings on transportation costs.
Regional Pass Lake Geneva-Alps	76	3, 4, 6, or 8 days	Unlimited travel in the region, including trains, buses, boats, and some mountain railways.	Great for exploring the Lake Geneva and Alps region.

Tell-Pass	110	2, 3, 4, 5, or 10 days	Unlimited travel on the Swiss Travel System network and free access to many mountain railways and cable cars.	Ideal for exploring the Lake Lucerne and Uri region.
Jungfrau Travel Pass	120	3, 4, 5, 6, 7, or 15 days	Unlimited travel in the Jungfrau region, including trains, buses, and boats, plus free access to mountain railways and cable cars.	Perfect for those exploring the Jungfrau mountain region.

Postal Bus Excursions

The train isn't the only way to see Switzerland's epic mountains. Postal bus excursions in Switzerland offer a cheap and unique picturesque way to explore the stunning landscapes, charming villages, and winding mountain roads of the country. Operated by Swiss PostBus (PostAuto), these excursions provide travelers with the opportunity to experience Switzerland's beauty while enjoying the convenience of public transportation and they are super cheap. A Three Day Pass Bus tour costs CHF 105. The main benefits, beyond it being a super deal are:

Scenic Routes:
Postal bus routes take you through some of Switzerland's most scenic areas, including mountain passes, alpine valleys, and pristine lakes.

Quaint Villages:
The routes often include stops in picturesque villages where you can explore local culture, architecture, and perhaps enjoy a Swiss meal.

Comfortable Buses:
The buses are modern, comfortable, and equipped with large windows to ensure passengers get the best views.

Historical Routes:
Some postal bus routes have a historical significance, following paths that have connected remote regions for centuries.

Booking options can be found here: https://www.postauto.ch/en/leisure-offers/excursion-tips

Free Museums

Switzerland has a variety of museums showcasing its rich cultural heritage. While many museums have an entrance fee, some offer free entry on specific days or times. Here are a few notable museums and tips on visiting for free:

Swiss National Museum (Landesmuseum Zürich):
Free Entry: The museum offers free admission on the first Sunday of each month.

Kunsthaus Zürich (Zurich Art Museum):
Free Entry: Every Wednesday from 4 pm, admission to the collection is free.

Museum of Art and History (Musée d'Art et d'Histoire), Geneva: Free Entry: Admission is free on the first Sunday of each month.

Bern Historical Museum (Bernisches Historisches Museum): Free Entry: The museum offers free admission on the first Thursday of each month from 5 pm to 9 pm.

Basel Art Museum (Kunstmuseum Basel):
Free Entry: On the last Saturday of every month, the museum offers free admission.

International Red Cross and Red Crescent Museum, Geneva:
Free Entry: Every first Sunday of the month, admission is free.

Swiss Museum Pass: Consider purchasing the Swiss Museum Pass (from 166 CHF for the year), which provides free entry to numerous museums across the country. It's valid for a certain period and can be cost-effective if you plan to visit multiple museums.

City Cards: Before you enter a museum, check if it would be cheaper to buy a Swiss ctourist cards that include free or discounted entry to local museums. Nearly every city in Switzerland has them.

Take Lake Boat Tours

Each Swiss lake is a reflective mirror set amidst the Alpine tapestry, capturing the essence of Switzerland's natural allure in a serene water ballet. There is no better way to experience the lakes, then on a boat tours. Here are a couple of super affordable ones:

Lake Geneva Boat Tours:
Boat tours on Lake Geneva offer stunning views of the Alps and lakeside towns. Prices for basic tours can start around CHF 20-30, while longer or more specialized tours may cost more.

Lake Lucerne Boat Tours:
Explore the beauty of Lake Lucerne with boat tours that often include narrated commentary on the surrounding areas. Prices can range from CHF 30-50 for standard tours.

Lake Zurich Boat Tours:
Boat tours on Lake Zurich provide a scenic experience with views of the city and the Swiss Alps. Prices for standard tours may start around CHF 15-25.

Go on Watch Making Tours

Switzerland is renowned for its watchmaking heritage, and several watchmaking tours offer an immersive experience into this craftsmanship. Here are some of the best watchmaking tours in Switzerland. Prices are actually really cheap, averaging 10 CHF

Patek Philippe Museum, Geneva:
Explore the Patek Philippe Museum in Geneva, showcasing the history of watchmaking and featuring an impressive collection of timepieces. The museum provides insights into Patek Philippe's craftsmanship.

Omega Museum and Factory Tour, Biel/Bienne:
Omega offers guided tours of its museum and factory in Biel/Bienne. Witness the production process, see historical timepieces, and learn about Omega's significant contributions to watchmaking.

Audemars Piguet Museum and Manufacture, Le Brassus:
Audemars Piguet, located in Le Brassus, offers tours of its museum and manufacturing facilities. Explore the craftsmanship behind Audemars Piguet watches, including the iconic Royal Oak.

Vacheron Constantin, Geneva:
Vacheron Constantin provides private tours of its Geneva-based Maison. Discover the brand's history, see master watchmakers at work, and admire Vacheron Constantin's exquisite timepieces.

Jaeger-LeCoultre Manufacture, Vallée de Joux:
Jaeger-LeCoultre offers tours of its manufacture in Vallée de Joux. Visitors can witness the various stages of watch production, from design to assembly, and explore the brand's innovations.

Swatch Pavillon, Biel/Bienne:
The Swatch Group offers tours at the Swatch Pavillon in Biel/Bienne. Learn about the history of Swatch and the brand's impact on the watch industry. The tour includes a visit to the production facilities.

Longines Museum and Factory Tour, Saint-Imier:
Longines, located in Saint-Imier, welcomes visitors to its museum and offers guided tours of its factory. Gain insights into the precision and craftsmanship behind Longines timepieces.

IWC Schaffhausen, Manufakturzentrum:
IWC Schaffhausen provides guided tours of its Manufakturzentrum. Explore the production areas and witness the intricate process of creating IWC watches.

Visit Churches

Switzerland is home to numerous churches with rich histories and remarkable architecture. Entry to at least parts of the church is typically free. Here are some notable churches in Switzerland, along with a glimpse of their history and highlights:

Grossmünster, Zurich:
History: One of Zurich's four major churches, Grossmünster has Romanesque origins and played a significant role in the Protestant Reformation.
Highlights: Climb the tower for panoramic views of Zurich and explore the crypt with archaeological finds. Free with swiss travel pass or Zurich card.

St. Pierre Cathedral, Geneva:
History: St. Pierre Cathedral dates back to the 12th century and has been a place of worship for various denominations.
Highlights: Visit the archaeological site beneath the cathedral and climb the tower for stunning views of Geneva.

Cathedral of St. Ursus, Solothurn:
History: Solothurn Cathedral is a Baroque masterpiece, completed in the 18th century, with earlier foundations dating to the 9th century.
Highlights: Admire the Baroque architecture, the ornate interior, and the impressive organ.

Basilica of Notre-Dame, Geneva:
History: Built in the 19th century, the Basilica of Notre-Dame is a neo-Gothic church with a rich history.
Highlights: Explore the beautiful stained glass windows and the impressive pipe organ.

Cathedral of St. Mary and St. Nicholas, Fribourg:
History: Fribourg Cathedral is a Gothic masterpiece dating back to the 13th century.
Highlights: Admire the Gothic architecture, the stunning stained glass windows, and the panoramic views from the tower.

Lausanne Cathedral, Lausanne:
History: Lausanne Cathedral is a major Gothic cathedral, begun in the 12th century.
Highlights: Visit the impressive rose window, the organ, and the archaeological site beneath the cathedral.

St. John's Church, Bern:
History: St. John's Church is a Protestant church with origins in the 15th century.
Highlights: Explore the interior with its medieval frescoes and the beautiful stained glass windows.

Minster of Basel, Basel:
History: Basel Minster is a Gothic cathedral with construction dating back to the 9th century.
Highlights: Climb the tower for breathtaking views of Basel and explore the interior with its impressive sculptures.

Free bike Hire

Picture this: you are cruising along the cobblestone streets, the gentle hum of the city blending with the soft whirr of your bike wheels. In cities like Zurich and Geneva, cycling is practically an art form. You'll find dedicated bike lanes that weave through charming neighborhoods and alongside serene lakeshores. Take a leisurely ride along the Limmat River in Zurich, or pedal through the Parc La Bâtie in Geneva for a breath of fresh air. The best part? You'll feel like a local and there are so many free schemes:

Zurich:
Zurich has a bike-sharing program called "Züri rollt," providing free bikes at various locations. The first hour is usually free, and charges apply for longer usage.
Geneva:
Geneva's "Genèveroule" offers free bike rentals for up to four hours. You can find bike stations throughout the city.
Lausanne:
Lausanne provides free "Lausanne Roule" bikes for up to four hours. The program is aimed at promoting sustainable transportation.
Basel:
"Velodi" in Basel offers free bikes for up to four hours. The system includes both regular bikes and e-bikes.
Bern:
Bern offers "Bern rollt" bikes for free for up to four hours. The program aims to encourage residents and visitors to explore the city on two wheels.
Fribourg:
The "LiberoBike" scheme in Fribourg provides free bikes for up to four hours, allowing you to discover the city and its surroundings.

Indulge in Outlet Shopping

Switzerland is home to several outlet shopping destinations where you can find discounted prices on a variety of designer and brand-name items. Here are some of the best outlet shopping locations in Switzerland:

FoxTown Outlet - Mendrisio:
Located near Lugano, FoxTown Outlet is one of the largest outlet malls in Switzerland. It Offers a wide range of international and Italian luxury brands. Popular brands include Gucci, Prada, Versace, and more.

OUTLETCITY METZINGEN - Metzingen (near the Swiss border):
While technically in Germany, OUTLETCITY METZINGEN is conveniently located near the Swiss border. Features over 80 premium and luxury brands, including Hugo Boss, Michael Kors, and Adidas.

Landquart Fashion Outlet - Landquart:
Situated between Zurich and Chur, Landquart Fashion Outlet offers a variety of fashion, accessories, and lifestyle brands. Brands include Calvin Klein, Tommy Hilfiger, and Fossil.

La Vallée Village - Geneva:
Part of the Chic Outlet Shopping group, La Vallée Village is an open-air outlet shopping destination. Features high-end brands like Burberry, Jimmy Choo, and Valentino.

Schönenwerd Fashion Fish Outlet Shopping:
Located near Zurich, Fashion Fish Outlet Shopping offers discounts on various fashion and lifestyle brands.Brands include Diesel, Desigual, and Marc O'Polo.

Enjoy Breathtaking Mountain Cable Car Journeys

Switzerland offers some breathtaking cable car rides that provide stunning views of the Alps and picturesque landscapes. Here are a few notable cable car rides, along with tips on how to save money on them:

Titlis Rotair, Engelberg:
Experience the world's first revolving cable car with panoramic views of the Swiss Alps at Titlis Rotair.

Schilthorn Piz Gloria, Mürren:
Ascend to the iconic Piz Gloria revolving restaurant using the Schilthorn cable car, renowned for its James Bond film appearance.

Gornergrat Railway, Zermatt:
Take the Gornergrat Railway for stunning views of the Matterhorn.

Pilatus Railway, Lucerne:
Embark on the steepest cogwheel railway in the world with the Pilatus Railway.

Kleine Scheidegg - Jungfraujoch, Jungfrau Region:
Enjoy the mesmerizing journey to Jungfraujoch with cable cars and trains offering spectacular views of the Aletsch Glacier.

Stanserhorn CabriO, Stans:
Ride the Stanserhorn CabriO cable car featuring an open-air upper deck.

Flumserberg Cable Cars, Flumserberg:

Explore Flumserberg's cable cars for access to hiking trails and panoramic Swiss Alpine views.

Tips to Save Money on Cable Car Rides in Switzerland:

- **Check Online Discounts:** Many cable car operators offer discounted tickets for online purchases, so check the official websites in advance.
- **Travel Off-Peak:** Some cable cars have half price tickets after 4pm.
- **Group Discounts:** If you're traveling with a group, inquire about group discounts, which are common for cable cars in Switzerland.

Tips for an Unforgettable Mountain Experiences:

Sunrise and Sunset Magic: Experience the mountains during sunrise or sunset for magical lighting and fewer crowds. It's a photographer's dream and a serene time to enjoy the scenery.

Language Matters: Learn a few basic phrases in the local language. It enhances your experience and fosters connections with locals who appreciate the effort.

Avoid Peak Tourist Hours: Plan your visits to popular attractions during non-peak hours to enjoy a more relaxed atmosphere and capture stunning photos without the crowds.

Use Public Transportation Wisely: Invest in a Swiss Travel Pass, which includes free or discounted access to many cable cars and mountain railways.

Save on Top Attractions

Zermatt and the Matterhorn:

- Witness the iconic pyramid-shaped Matterhorn, a symbol of the Swiss Alps, and consider staying in nearby Tasch or Randa for an affordable experience.

Lucerne's Chapel Bridge and Lake Lucerne:

- Immerse yourself in Lucerne's medieval charm, take a leisurely stroll across Chapel Bridge, and consider a picnic along Lake Lucerne's shores.

Interlaken's Lakes and Mountains:

- Revel in the beauty of Interlaken, nestled between Lake Thun and Lake Brienz, and explore budget-friendly hiking options with breathtaking mountain views.

Jungfraujoch - Top of Europe:

- Reach the Jungfraujoch summit for a breathtaking panorama of glaciers and peaks. Consider visiting during non-peak hours to save on costs on cable cars.

Lauterbrunnen Valley's Waterfalls:

- Explore the magical Lauterbrunnen Valley, home to numerous waterfalls. Take advantage of the valley's free walking trails.

Bern's UNESCO Old Town:

- Discover Bern's UNESCO World Heritage site, the Old Town, and explore the city's charm on foot without additional costs.

Swiss National Park:

- Experience the unspoiled beauty of the Swiss National Park with budget-friendly hiking trails. Stay in nearby towns like Zernez for more economical accommodations.

Aletsch Glacier and Aletsch Arena:

- Marvel at the Aletsch Glacier, the Alps' largest, and save on expenses with budget-friendly cable cars and scenic trails in the Aletsch Arena.

The Jet d'Eau in Geneva:

- Admire the iconic Jet d'Eau fountain on Lake Geneva. Enjoy leisurely walks along the lakefront and explore the city's many free attractions.

Grindelwald's Alpine Charm:

- Experience the Alpine charm of Grindelwald and consider staying in the more affordable Grund area. Explore budget-friendly hiking trails for stunning views of the Jungfrau region.

Enjoy Luxury cheese, chocolate and wine experiences on a Budget

Switzerland, renowned for its rich culinary heritage, boasts a deep-seated love affair with three gastronomic treasures – cheese, chocolate, and wine. The Swiss have elevated cheese to an art form, producing an array of world-famous varieties such as Gruyère, Emmental, and Raclette. Cheese is not just a component of meals; it's a cultural icon, featured prominently in fondue gatherings and hearty Alpine dishes. Equally celebrated is Switzerland's mastery of chocolate craftsmanship, where velvety smooth and indulgent chocolates are created with meticulous attention to detail. Swiss chocolate has become synonymous with quality and sophistication, satisfying sweet cravings worldwide. Complementing these delectable treats is the Swiss dedication to winemaking. Nestled in the picturesque vineyards of regions like Valais and Lavaux, Swiss wines, though often underrated, showcase a diverse palette of flavors, mirroring the country's commitment to culinary excellence. The great news is, you can indulge cheaply!

Cheese Fondue in Gruyères:

Tip: Head to "Le Chalet" in Gruyères for an authentic and pocket-friendly fondue experience. Prices typically range from CHF 15 to CHF 30 per person.

History: Gruyères, nestled in the Fribourg region, is renowned for its namesake cheese, Gruyère. Dating back to the 12th century, the town's medieval charm enhances the flavors of its cheese fondue.

Wine Tasting in Lavaux Vineyards:

Tip: Explore the "Domaine Croix Duplex" winery in Lavaux for independent tastings against the backdrop of terraced vineyards. Tasting fees usually range from CHF 10 to CHF 20 per person.

History: The Lavaux region, a UNESCO World Heritage site on Lake Geneva, boasts a winemaking tradition dating back to the 12th century. The terraced vineyards showcase a breathtaking landscape shaped by centuries of viticulture.

Emmental Cheese Dairy Visit:

Tip: Visit "Schaukäserei Affoltern" for insightful tastings at an affordable price, often ranging from CHF 5 to CHF 15.

History: The Emmental region, recognized for its distinctive holed cheese, has a cheese-making heritage dating back to the early 13th century. Smaller dairies offer a genuine taste of tradition.

Wine & Cheese Pairing in Montreux:

Tip: Craft your own pairing adventure by selecting local wines and cheeses from the "Marché de Montreux" or "La Cave Vevey-Montreux." Prices for tip-friendly pairings may range from CHF 20 to CHF 40.

History: Nestled along the shores of Lake Geneva, Montreux has been a haven for artists and wine enthusiasts. The town's lively atmosphere complements the joy of discovering local wines and cheeses.

Appenzeller Cheese Experience:

Tip: Explore "Käserei Vogel" in the Appenzeller region for a taste of this unique cheese without breaking the bank. Prices for tastings may range from CHF 5 to CHF 15.

History: Appenzell has been crafting its distinctive cheese for over 700 years. Smaller producers provide an intimate look into the fascinating history and flavors of Appenzeller cheese.

Swiss Chocolate, Cheese, and Wine Tasting Events:

Tip: Attend the "Swiss Chocolate Chalet" events or the "Fête de l'Escalade" in Geneva for diverse tastings at a reasonable cost. Event entry fees can range from CHF 10 to CHF 30.

History: Switzerland's rich culinary history comes alive at these events, where enthusiasts gather to celebrate the country's delectable traditions. Enjoy a variety of flavors without breaking your tip.

Swiss Chocolate, Cheese, and Wine Tasting Events:

Tip: Attend events like those at the "Swiss Chocolate Chalet" or the "Fête de l'Escalade" in Geneva for diverse tastings. Event entry fees can range from CHF 10 to CHF 30.

History: Switzerland's culinary legacy unfolds at these events, providing a platform to celebrate the country's delectable traditions with chocolate, cheese, and wine.

Chocolate Experience in Zurich:

Tip: Explore the "Lindt Home of Chocolate" in Kilchberg, Zurich, for a fascinating chocolate experience. Entrance fees start at CHF 15.

History: Zurich, with its Lindt chocolate legacy, invites you to delve into the world of Swiss chocolate, uncovering a sweet history that dates back to the 19th century.

Enjoy Thermal Waters

Switzerland has a rich history of wellness dating back to the 19th century when the pristine Alpine air and natural landscapes began attracting visitors seeking health and relaxation. The Swiss Alps, with their clean mountain air, became synonymous with wellness and a retreat for those seeking a respite from the stresses of urban life. The concept of "air cures" gained popularity, with people believing in the therapeutic benefits of breathing in the pure mountain air for various respiratory and health conditions. Here are some super bargains on wellness:

Thermalbad & Spa Zurich:

Located in Zurich, this urban spa offers thermal baths and a wellness area. Prices for entry start around 35 to 45 Swiss Francs, depending on the time and day.

Tamina Therme, Bad Ragaz:

Bad Ragaz is known for its thermal waters, and Tamina Therme offers a variety of spa experiences. Entry prices typically start from around 30 to 40 Swiss Francs for the public baths.

Luxuriate in Parks and Gardens

Discover the opulence of Switzerland through the enchanting experience of exploring cost-free public parks and gardens in urban havens like Zurich, Geneva, and Bern.

Immerse yourself in the serene ambiance of Lugano's Parco Ciani, a picturesque lakeside retreat adorned with Mediterranean flora and captivating sculptures that beckon you to unwind and savor the beauty.

Embark on a journey to Bern's Bear Park, an open-air sanctuary designed to mimic the natural habitat of bears. Entrance is complimentary, allowing you to witness these majestic creatures in their element.

Partake in the vibrant tapestry of Swiss culture by attending various free public events and festivals held year-round. These celebrations showcase the richness of Swiss traditions, music, and cultural diversity.

Indulge your senses in the lush surroundings of botanical gardens, such as the Botanischer Garten Zurich, where diverse plant collections and expansive green spaces offer a delightful escape into nature's wonders.

Quench your thirst at the numerous Swiss water fountains scattered across cities. Not only is the water safe to drink, but it also comes without a price tag, adding a refreshing touch to your exploration of Switzerland's urban landscapes.

Visit Waterfalls

Switzerland is home to some stunning waterfalls, and visiting them can be an amazing experience. Here are the following waterfalls and some tips for budget-friendly travel:

Rhine Falls:
    Location: Near the town of Schaffhausen.
    How to Visit Cheaply: Use public transportation to get to Schaffhausen and then take a local bus to the falls. Consider purchasing a regional travel pass for cost savings.
    Cheap Eats Nearby: Look for local bakeries or grocery stores in Schaffhausen for affordable snacks.

Trümmelbach Falls:
    Location: In the Lauterbrunnen Valley.
    How to Visit Cheaply: Consider purchasing a Jungfrau Travel Pass, which covers transportation in the region. Utilize budget accommodations in nearby towns like Lauterbrunnen.
    Cheap Eats Nearby: Explore cafes or markets in Lauterbrunnen for more affordable food options.

Staubbach Falls:
    Location: Also in Lauterbrunnen Valley, near the village of Lauterbrunnen.
    How to Visit Cheaply: Similar to Trümmelbach Falls, use a regional pass for transportation and choose budget-friendly accommodations.
    Cheap Eats Nearby: Check out local restaurants in Lauterbrunnen that cater to a range of budgets.

Giessbach Falls:
    Location: On the shores of Lake Brienz.
    How to Visit Cheaply: Use boat services on Lake Brienz for a scenic and cost-effective approach. Look for budget accommodations in nearby towns like Interlaken.
    Cheap Eats Nearby: Explore eateries in Interlaken for a variety of dining options.

Engstligen Falls:
    Location: Near the town of Adelboden.
    How to Visit Cheaply: Utilize public transportation to Adelboden and then consider hiking to the falls to save on additional transport costs.
    Cheap Eats Nearby: Look for local cafes or smaller restaurants in Adelboden for more affordable meals.

Visit Underrated villages

Switzerland is dotted with charming villages that offer a more tranquil and authentic experience compared to popular tourist destinations. Here are some underrated villages, along with tips on how to enjoy a luxury stay on a budget:

Lauterbrunnen:
    Underrated Charm: Nestled in a picturesque valley with 72 waterfalls, Lauterbrunnen is often overshadowed by nearby Interlaken. It serves as an excellent base for exploring the Jungfrau region.
    Budget Luxury Stay: Look for boutique hotels, guesthouses, or self-catering accommodations. Booking in advance and during the shoulder seasons can often yield much lower rates.

Saas Fee:
    Underrated Charm: Saas Fee is a car-free village surrounded by stunning Alpine peaks. It offers a quieter alternative to the more popular Zermatt.
    Budget Luxury Stay: Explore package deals that include accommodation and activities. Consider staying slightly outside the village center for more affordable options while still enjoying the surrounding beauty.

Zeneggen:
    Underrated Charm: Zeneggen is a small mountain village with traditional Swiss chalets and panoramic views of the Valais Alps.
    Budget Luxury Stay: Explore family-run guesthouses or bed and breakfasts for a more personalized experience. Take advantage of local dining options for authentic and budget-friendly meals.

Guarda:
    Underrated Charm: Guarda, in the Engadin region, is known for its well-preserved Engadine houses. It offers a glimpse into traditional Swiss mountain life.
    Budget Luxury Stay: Opt for guesthouses or inns for a cozy experience. Consider booking directly with accommodation providers for potential discounts.

Stein am Rhein:
    Underrated Charm: This medieval town is located on the shores of the Rhine River, featuring well-preserved half-timbered houses and cobblestone streets.

Aigle:
    Underrated Charm: Aigle is known for its medieval castle and vineyards, offering a quieter alternative to larger Swiss towns.
    Budget Luxury Stay: Consider staying in a boutique hotel or guesthouse. Take advantage of local vineyard tours and wine tastings for a touch of luxury.

Explore Caves

Switzerland is home to some fascinating caves that offer unique geological formations and experiences. While some caves may not be specifically considered "luxurious," you can enhance your visit with guided tours and find budget-friendly accommodations nearby. Here are a few caves to consider:

St. Beatus Caves (St. Beatus-Höhlen):

Location: Near Lake Thun, Interlaken.
Guided Tours: The St. Beatus Caves offer guided tours that take you through a series of underground chambers with stalactites and stalagmites. Tours are available in several languages.
Budget Luxury Stay: Look for accommodations in nearby towns like Interlaken or Thun. Consider smaller guesthouses or bed and breakfasts for a more personalized experience.

Reichenbach Falls Cave (Reichenbachfallhöhle):

Location: Near Meiringen.
Guided Tours: The Reichenbach Falls Cave is part of the Sherlock Holmes experience in the area. While the cave itself is relatively small, the guided tour includes information about the famous fictional detective Sherlock Holmes.
Budget Luxury Stay: Explore accommodations in Meiringen or nearby towns. Look for charming Swiss chalets or guesthouses that offer a cozy atmosphere.

Wildkirchli Cave (Wildkirchlihöhle):

Location: Ebenalp, Appenzell.
Guided Tours: The Wildkirchli Cave is part of the famous Aescher Cliff area. Guided tours take you through the cave, showcasing its geological features. It's also known for its prehistoric findings.
Budget Luxury Stay: Consider staying in nearby Appenzell or Wasserauen. Look for family-run inns or guesthouses that provide a unique Swiss experience.

Hölloch Cave:

Location: Muotathal, Schwyz.
Guided Tours: Hölloch Cave is one of the longest cave systems in Europe. While not typically associated with luxury, guided tours are available to explore certain sections of the cave.
Budget Luxury Stay: Look for accommodations in Muotathal or nearby Schwyz. While luxury options may be limited, you can find cozy inns or guesthouses that offer a comfortable stay.

Trümmelbach Falls Caves:

Location: Lauterbrunnen Valley.

Guided Tours: Trümmelbach Falls is a series of impressive waterfalls inside a mountain. While not a traditional cave, the underground tunnels and chambers are accessible via guided tours, showcasing the power of melting glaciers.

Budget Luxury Stay: Explore accommodations in Lauterbrunnen or nearby towns like Wengen. Look for options with views of the surrounding mountains.

Enjoy Cow Parades

Cow parades are popular in regions where dairy farming is prominent. These parades often feature elaborately decorated cows adorned with flowers and other ornaments, and they celebrate the return of the cows from their summer pastures in the mountains. Here are some of the best-known cow parades in Switzerland:

Züri Fäscht Cow Parade (Zurich):
Zurich hosts a massive city festival called Züri Fäscht, during which a cow parade is often organized. The parade includes beautifully decorated cows and attracts both locals and tourists. Check the Züri Fäscht event schedule for information on the cow parade during the festival.

Eidgenössisches Jodlerfest (Swiss Yodeling Festival):
The Swiss Yodeling Festival, held every three years in different locations, often features a cow parade as part of the festivities. It's a great opportunity to experience Swiss traditions, including yodeling, traditional music, and beautifully decorated cows.

Engstlenalp Cow Descent (Bernese Oberland):
Engstlenalp, located in the Bernese Oberland, hosts an annual cow descent festival where cows return from the high alpine pastures to lower altitudes for the winter. The cows are adorned with flowers, and there are festivities to celebrate the occasion.

Alpabfahrt in Appenzell (Appenzell):
The region of Appenzell is known for its picturesque landscapes and traditional events, including Alpabfahrt (cow descent). The cows are beautifully decorated, and the event is a colorful spectacle. Check the local calendar for details on the specific dates.

Alpabzug in Charmey (Fribourg):
Charmey, in the canton of Fribourg, hosts a charming cow parade during its Alpabzug. The event includes traditional music, local crafts, and, of course, beautifully adorned cows making their way down from the alpine pastures.

La Poya des Vaches (Gruyères):
Gruyères, famous for its cheese, hosts La Poya des Vaches, a cow parade celebrating the return of the cows from the mountain pastures. The parade is accompanied by folk music and local festivities.

How to Enjoy ALLOCATING Money in Switzerland

'Money's greatest intrinsic value—and this can't be overstated—is its ability to give you control over your time.' - Morgan Housel

Notice I have titled the chapter how to enjoy allocating money in Switzerland. I'll use saving and allocating interchangeably in the book, but since most people associate saving to feel like a turtleneck, that's too tight, I've chosen to use wealth language. Rich people don't save. They allocate. What's the difference? Saving can feel like something you don't want or wish to do and allocating has your personal will attached to it.

And on that note, it would be helpful if you considered removing the following words and phrase from your vocabulary for planning and enjoying your Switzerland trip:

- Wish
- Want
- Maybe someday

These words are part of poverty language. Language is a dominant source of creation. Use it to your advantage. You don't have to wish, want or say maybe someday to Switzerland. You can enjoy the same things millionaires enjoy in Switzerland without the huge spend.

'People don't like to be sold-but they love to buy.' - Jeffrey Gitomer.

Every good salesperson who understands the quote above places obstacles in the way of their clients' buying. Companies create waiting lists, restaurants pay people to queue outside in order to create demand. People reason if something is so in demand, it must be worth having but that's often just marketing. Take this sales maxim 'People don't like to be sold-but they love to buy and flip it on its head to allocate your money in Switzerland on things YOU desire. You love to spend and hate to be sold. That means when something comes your way, it's not 'I can't afford it,' it's 'I don't want it' or maybe 'I don't want it right now'.

Saving money doesn't mean never buying a latte, never taking a taxi, never taking vacations (of course, you bought this book). Only you get to decide on how you spend and on what. Not an advice columnist who thinks you can buy a house if you never eat avocado toast again.

I love what Kate Northrup says about affording something: "If you really wanted it you would figure out a way to get it. If it were that VALUABLE to you, you would make it happen."

I believe if you master the art of allocating money to bargains, it can feel even better than spending it! Bold claim, I know. But here's the truth: Money gives you freedom and options. The more you keep in your account and or invested the more freedom and options you'll have. The principal reason you should save and allocate money is TO BE FREE! Remember, a trip's main purpose is relaxation, rest and enjoyment, aka to feel free.

When you talk to most people about saving money on vacation. They grimace. How awful they proclaim not to go wild on your vacation. If you can't get into a ton of debt enjoying your once-in-a-lifetime vacation, when can you?

When you spend money 'theres's a sudden rush of dopamine which vanishes once the transaction is complete. What happens in the brain when you save money? It increases feelings of security and peace. You don't need to stress life's uncertainties. And having a greater sense of peace can actually help you save more money.' Stressed out people make impulsive financial choices, calm people don't.'

The secret to enjoying saving money on vacation is very simple: never save money from a position of lack. Don't think 'I wish I could afford that'. Choose not to be marketed to. Choose not to consume at a price others set. Don't save money from the flawed premise you don't have enough. Don't waste your time living in the box that society has created, which says saving money on vacation means sacrifice. It doesn't.

Traveling to Switzerland can be an expensive endeavor if you don't approach it with a plan, but you have this book which is packed with tips. The biggest other asset is your perspective.

How to feel RICH in Switzerland

While Switzerland had an average wealth per adult of around $714,000 USD, ranking it among the top countries in terms of average wealth, you don't need millions in your bank to **feel rich**. Feeling rich feels different to every person."Researchers have pooled data on the relationship between money and emotions from more than 1.6 million people across 162 countries and found that **wealthier people feel more positive "self-regard emotions" such as confidence, pride and determination."**

Here are things to see, do and taste in Switzerland, that will have you overflowing with gratitude for your luxury trip to Switzerland.

- Achieving a Michelin Star rating is the most coveted accolade for restaurants but those that obtain a Michelin Star are synonymous with high cost, but in Switzerland there are restaurants with Michelin-stars offering lunch menus for 15 euros or less!If you want to taste the finest seasonal local dishes while dining in pure luxury, visit Ron Blaauw's Gastrobar to indulge in an unforgettable treat. If fine dining isn't your thing, don't worry further on in the guide you will find a range of delicious cheap eats in Switzerland that deserve a Michelin-Star.
- While money can't buy happiness, it can buy cake and isn't that sort of the same thing? Jokes aside, these bakeries have turned cakes and pastries into edible art.
  - **Sprüngli in Zurich:** Famous for its Luxemburgerli macarons and high-quality pastries.
  - **Bäckerei Fleischli in Zurich:** Known for its traditional Swiss bread and pastries.
  - **Toni's in St. Gallen:** Renowned for its exquisite bread and pastries, including the "Olma-Brötli."
  - **Confiserie Bachmann in Lucerne:** Offers a variety of Swiss pastries, cakes, and chocolates.
  - **Felsenau Bäckerei-Konditorei in Bern:** Well-regarded for its artisanal bread and pastries.
- While you might not be staying in a penthouse, you can still enjoy the same views. Visit rooftop bars in Switzerland, like **Harder Kulm in Interlaken:** Accessible by funicular, it offers a stunning perspective of the Jungfrau region.

Those are just some ideas for you to know that visiting Switzerland on a budget doesn't have to feel like sacrifice or constriction. Now let's get into the nuts and bolts of Switzerland on the super cheap.

How to use this book

Google and TripAdvisor are your on-the-go guides while traveling, a travel guide adds the most value during the planning phase, and if you're without Wi-Fi. Always download the google map for your destination - having an offline map will make using this guide much more comfortable. For ease of use, we've set the book out the way you travel, booking your flights, arriving, how to get around, then on to the money-saving tips. The tips we ordered according to when you need to know the tip to save money, so free tours and combination tickets feature first. We prioritized the rest of the tips by how much money you can save and then by how likely it was that you could find the tip with a google search. Meaning those we think you could find alone are nearer the bottom. I hope you find this layout useful. If you have any ideas about making Super Cheap Insider Guides easier to use, please email me philgattang@gmail.com

A quick note on How We Source Super Cheap Tips
We focus entirely on finding the best bargains. We give each of our collaborators $2,000 to hunt down never-before-seen deals. The type you either only know if you're local or by on the ground research. We spend zero on marketing and a little on designing an excellent cover. We do this yearly, which means we just keep finding more amazing ways for you to have the same experience for less.

Now let's get started with juicing the most pleasure from your trip to Switzerland with the least possible money!

The 26 cantons of Switzerland

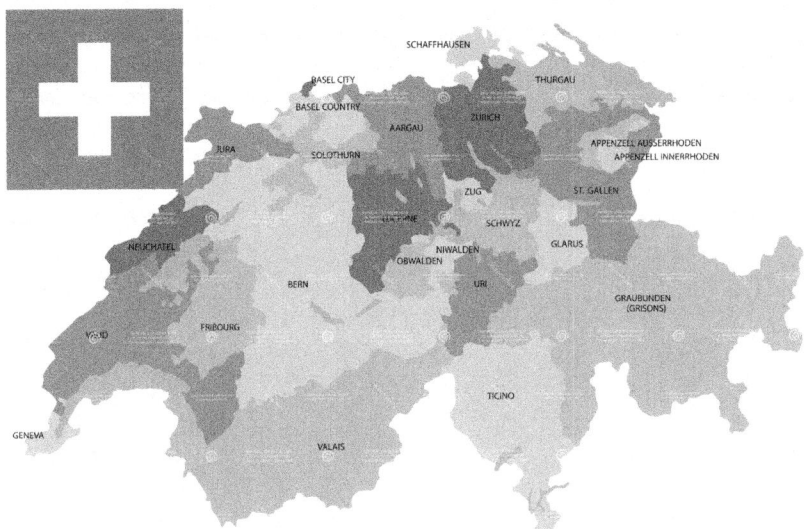

Swiss cantons

Switzerland is divided into 26 cantons, each of which functions as a semi-autonomous region with its own constitution, government, and parliament. Here's a brief overview of how the cantonal system works in Switzerland:

Switzerland is all about that autonomy game! Each canton here has a ton of independence, dealing with everything not explicitly given to the federal government by the Swiss Constitution. That's a hefty responsibility, covering education, health, police, and even the local transportation scene.

Now, get this: every canton is like its own little kingdom with its own constitution – yup, you heard it right, its own rulebook. They've got to make sure it jives with the Swiss Federal Constitution, though. Can't have any constitutional clashes, you know?
So, picture this: each canton's got its own set of rulers. There's the executive branch, often a government or council, and the legislative branch, think parliament or assembly. They're the big shots responsible for putting laws into action and making sure everything runs smoothly on the cantonal level.

And don't even get me started on cantonal parliaments. These guys are the real decision-makers within their borders. They're the ones having heated debates and giving the nod to laws that impact the canton directly.

But here's the catch – the cantons can't just go wild. They can make their own laws, sure, but they can't go against the Swiss Federal Constitution or federal laws. Gotta keep things in check, right?

Now, here's where it gets interesting. Cantons are like buddies who help each other out. They team up through these cool inter-cantonal agreements, making sure they're all on the same page on issues that stretch across their borders. It's like Switzerland saying, "We got this, together!"

So, in a nutshell, Switzerland's cantonal system that's all about balance. They've figured out how to have a strong federal game while still respecting the unique flavors of each region – be it in language, culture, or history.

Planning your trip

When to visit

The first step in saving money on your Switzerland trip is timing. If you are not tied to school holidays, the **best time to visit is during the shoulder-season months of March, April and October and November.**

Traveling in the off-season offers a host of benefits. You will have less of a chance to be jostled by large crowds and your hotel bookings will be much cheaper and you won't need to buy skip the line tickets. Plus, during these shoulder months, there is a chance of seeing tulips in bloom. In addition, you will find some of the Netherlands' most scenic beaches and small towns.

The High season starts in April and goes until September and prices DOUBLE so if you're planning to come then book accommodation ahead of time to save money on price hikes.

If you are visiting during the peak season, you should expect to pay higher rates for hotels and airfare. You will also have to cope with long lines at some of the city's most popular attractions but don't despair there are innumerable hacks to save on accommodation in Switzerland which we will go into detail on. Plus if you visit in summer, Switzerland is awash with free festivals. From the Robeco Zomerconcerten series to the Vondelpark Open Air Theater, there's something for everyone.

Seasons

Switzerland experiences distinct seasons, each offering unique opportunities for exploration. Here's a guide on what to pack for each season:

- Spring (March to May):
    - **Clothing:** Light layers, including a jacket or sweater, as temperatures can vary. Comfortable walking shoes for exploring.
    - **Accessories:** An umbrella and a hat for occasional rain.
- Summer (June to August):
    - **Clothing:** T-shirts, shorts, and lightweight pants. A light jacket or sweater for cooler evenings. Comfortable walking shoes for outdoor activities.
    - **Accessories:** Sunglasses, sunscreen, and a hat. If you're planning mountain activities, pack hiking boots.
- Autumn (September to November):
    - **Clothing:** Similar to spring, with layers. A waterproof jacket and warmer layers as temperatures cool down.
    - **Accessories:** A scarf and gloves for cooler days. Consider sturdy shoes for autumn walks.
- Winter (December to February):
    - **Clothing:** Heavy, insulated jacket, thermal layers, gloves, and a hat. Waterproof boots for snow. Pack warm socks and thermal undergarments if you plan on spending time outdoors.

- **Accessories:** A scarf and earmuffs for added warmth. Snow gear if you intend to engage in winter sports.

Free Events

Month	Event	Description	Approximate Month/Date
January	Basel Fasnacht (Carnival)	Colorful parades, costumes, and festivities.	February/March
July/Aug	Geneva Festival (Fêtes de Genève)	Celebrations around Lake Geneva with events, concerts, and fireworks.	Late July to Early August
July	Montreux Jazz Festival	Internationally renowned jazz festival.	July
August	Street Parade in Zurich	One of the largest techno parties in the world.	August
August 1	National Day (Bundesfeier)	Celebrations across the country with parades and fireworks.	August 1
September/October	Zurich Film Festival	Film screenings, discussions, and events.	September/October
November to December	Lausanne Festival of Lights	Winter festival with light installations and performances.	November to December
May	Swiss National Museum Day (Museumstag)	Many museums offer free or discounted entry.	May

Booking Flights

How to Find Heavily Discounted Private Jet Flights to or from Switzerland

If you're dreaming of travelling to Switzerland on a private jet you can accomplish your dream for a 10th of the cost.

Empty leg flights, also known as empty leg charters or deadhead flights, are flights operated by private jet companies that do not have any passengers on board. These flights occur when a private jet is chartered for a one-way trip, but the jet needs to return to its base or another location without passengers.

Rather than flying empty, private jet companies may offer these empty leg flights for a reduced price to travelers who are flexible and able to fly on short notice. Because the flight is already scheduled and paid for by the original charter, private jet companies are willing to offer these flights at a discounted rate in order to recoup some of the cost.

Empty leg flights can be a cost-effective way to experience the luxury and convenience of private jet travel.

Taking an empty leg private jet flight from America to Switzerland

The New York City-Zurich route is one of the busiest private jet routes in the world, with many private jet operators offering regular flights between the two cities.

There are several websites that offer empty leg flights for booking. Here are a few:

JetSuiteX: This website offers discounted, last-minute flights on private jets, including empty leg flights.

PrivateFly: This website allows you to search for empty leg flights by location or date. You can also request a quote for a custom flight if you have specific needs.

Victor: This website offers a variety of private jet services, including empty leg flights.

Sky500: This website offers a variety of private jet services, including empty leg flights.

Air Charter Service: This website allows you to search for empty leg flights by location or date. You can also request a quote for a custom flight if you have specific needs.

Keep in mind that empty leg flights are often available at short notice, so it's a good idea to be flexible with your travel plans if you're looking for a deal. It's also important to do your research and read reviews before booking a flight with any company.

RECAP: To book an empty leg flight in Switzerland, follow these steps:

1. Research and identify private jet companies and or brokers that offer empty leg flights departing from Switzerland. You can use the websites mentioned earlier, such as JetSuiteX, PrivateFly, Victor, Sky500, or Air Charter Service, to search for available flights.

2. Check the availability and pricing of empty leg flights that match your travel dates and destination. Empty leg flights are often available at short notice.

3. Contact the private jet company or broker to inquire about booking the empty leg flight. Be sure to provide your travel details, including your preferred departure and arrival times, number of passengers, and any special requests.

4. Confirm your booking and make payment. Private jet companies and brokers typically require full payment upfront, so be prepared to pay for the flight in advance.

5. Arrive at the airport at least 30 minutes before the scheduled departure time.

6. Check in at the private jet terminal and go through any necessary security checks. Unlike commercial airlines, there is typically no long queue or security checks for private jet flights.

7. Board the private jet and settle into your seat. You will have plenty of space to stretch out and relax, as well as access to amenities such as Wi-Fi, entertainment systems, and refreshments.

How to Find CHEAP FIRST-CLASS Flights to Switzerland

Upgrade at the airport

Airlines are extremely reluctant to advertise price drops in first or business class tickets so the best way to secure them is actually at the airport when airlines have no choice but to decrease prices dramatically because otherwise they lose money. Ask about upgrading to business or first-class when you check-in. If you check-in online look around the airport for your airlines branded bidding system.

Use Air-miles

When it comes to accruing air-miles for American citizens **Chase Sapphire Reserve card** ranks top. If you put everything on there and pay it off immediately you will end up getting free flights all the time, aside from taxes.

Get 2-3 chase cards with sign up bonuses, you'll have 200k points in no time and can book with points on multiple airlines when transferring your points to them.

Please note, this is only applicable to those living in the USA. In the Bonus Section we have detailed the best air-mile credit cards for those living in other countries.

How many miles does it take to fly first class?
New York City to Switzerland could require anywhere from 70,000 to 120,000 frequent flyer miles, depending on the airline and the time of year you plan to travel.

How to Fly Business Class to Switzerland cheaply

TAP Air Portugal is a popular airline that operates flights from New York City to Zurich with the cheapest business class options. In low season this route typically started at around $400-$1,500 per person for a round-trip ticket.

To find the best deals on business class flights to Switzerland, follow these steps:

1. Use travel search engines: Start by searching for flights on popular travel search engines like Google Flights, Kayak, or Skyscanner. These sites allow you to compare prices from different airlines and book the cheapest available business option.
2. Sign up for airline newsletters: Airlines often send out exclusive deals and promotions to their email subscribers. Sign up for TAP Air Portugal's newsletter to receive notifications about special offers and discounts on business class flights.
3. Book in advance: Booking your flight well in advance can help you secure a better deal on business class tickets. Aim to book your flight at least two to three months before your travel date.

Cheapest route to Switzerland from America

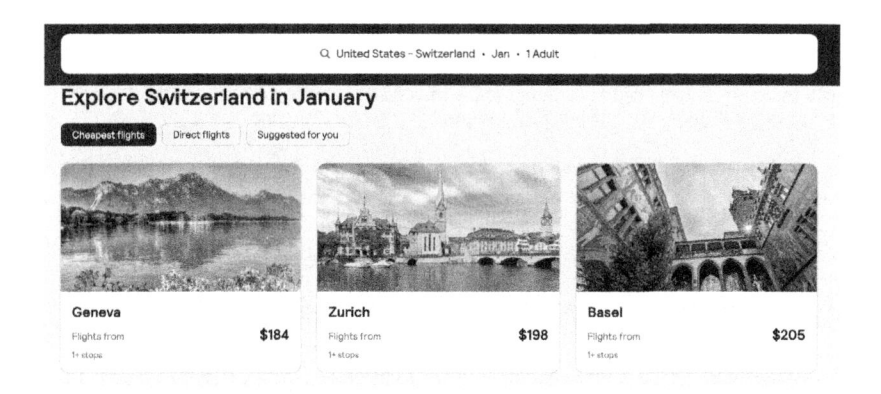

Explore Switzerland in January

Geneva	Zurich	Basel
Flights from $184	Flights from $198	Flights from $205
1+ stops	1+ stops	1+ stops

You can flights from the states to Geneva for under $200. The best budget Airlines include Norse Atlantic, Wizz Air, Easyjet and British Airways for this route.

If you can't find a good deal for your dates, look into flying into an alternate European hub and then taking a budget airline or train to Switzerland. Popular nearby hubs include Frankfurt, Munich, or Milan.

How to ALWAYS Find Super Cheap Flights to Switzerland

If you're just interested in finding the cheapest flight to Switzerland here is here to do it!

Luck is just an illusion.

Anyone can find incredible flight deals. If you can be flexible you can save huge amounts of money. In fact, the biggest tip I can give you for finding incredible flight deals is simple: find a flexible job. Don't despair if you can't do that theres still a lot you can do.

Book your flight to Switzerland on a Tuesday or Wednesday

Tuesdays and Wednesdays are the cheapest days of the week to fly. You can take a flight to Switzerland on a Tuesday or Wednesday for less than half the price you'd pay on a Thursday Friday, Saturday, Sunday or Monday.

Start with Google Flights (but NEVER book through them)

I conduct upwards of 50 flight searches a day for readers. I use google flights first when looking for flights. I put specific departure but broad destination (e.g Europe) and usually find amazing deals.

The great thing about Google Flights is you can search by class. You can pick a specific destination and it will tell you which time is cheapest in which class. Or you can put in dates and you can see which area is cheapest to travel to.

But be aware Google flights does not show the cheapest prices among the flight search engines but it does offer several advantages

1. You can see the cheapest dates for the next 8 weeks. Other search engines will blackout over 70% of the prices.
2. You can put in multiple airports to fly from. Just use a common to separate in the from input.
3. If you're flexible on where you're going Google flights can show you the cheapest destinations.
4. You can set-up price tracking, where Google will email you when prices rise or decline.

Once you have established the cheapest dates to fly go over to skyscanner.net and put those dates in. You will find sky scanner offers the cheapest flights.

Get Alerts when Prices to Switzerland are Lowest

Google also has a nice feature which allows you to set up an alert to email you when prices to your destination are at their lowest. So if you don't have fixed dates this feature can save you a fortune.

Baggage add-ons

It may be cheaper and more convenient to send your luggage separately with a service like sendmybag.com Often the luggage sending fee is cheaper than what the airlines charge to check baggage. Visit Lugless.com or luggagefree.com in addition to sendmybag.com for a quotation.

Loading times

Anyone who has attempted to find a cheap flight will know the pain of excruciating long loading times. If you encounter this issue use google flights to find the cheapest dates and then go to skyscanner.net for the lowest price.

Always try to book direct with the airline

Once you have found the cheapest flight go direct to the airlines booking page. This is advantageous because if you need to change your flights or arrange a refund, its much easier to do so, than via a third party booking agent.

That said, sometimes the third party bookers offer cheaper deals than the airline, so you need to make the decision based on how likely you think it is that disruption will impede you making those flights.

More Fight Tricks and Tips

www.secretflying.com/usa-deals offers a range of deals from the USA and other countries. For example you can pick-up a round trip flight non-stop from from the east coast to johannesburg for $350 return on this site

Scott's cheap flights, you can select your home airport and get emails on deals but you pay for an annual subscription. A free workaround is to download Hopper and set search alerts for trips/price drops.

Premium service of Scott's cheap flights.
They sometime have discounted business and first class but in my experience they are few and far between.

JGOOT.com has 5 times as many choices as Scott's cheap flights.

kiwi.com allows you to be able to do radius searches so you can find cheaper flights to general areas.

Finding Error Fares

Travel Pirates (www.travelpirates.com) is a gold-mine for finding error deals. Subscribe to their newsletter. I recently found a reader an airfare from Montreal-Brazil for a $200 round trip (mistake fare!). Of course these error fares are always certain dates, but if you can be flexible you can save a lot of money.

Things you can do that might reduce the fare to Switzerland:

- Use a VPN (if the booker knows you booked one-way, the return fare will go up)
- Buy your ticket in a different currency

If all else fails...

If you can't find a cheap flight for your dates I can find one for you. I do not charge for this nor do I send affiliate links. I'll send you a screenshot of the best options I find as airlines attach cookies to flight links. To use this free service please review this guide and send me a screenshot of your review - with your flight hacking request. I aim to reply to you within 12 hours. If it's an urgent request mark the email URGENT in the subject line and I will endeavour to reply ASAP.

A tip for coping with Jet-lag

Jetlag is primarily caused by disruptions to the body's circadian rhythm, which is the internal "biological clock" that regulates many of the body's processes, including sleep-wake cycles. When you travel across multiple time zones, your body's clock is disrupted, leading to symptoms like fatigue, insomnia, and stomach problems.

Eating on your travel destination's time before you travel can help to adjust your body's clock before you arrive, which can help to mitigate the effects of jetlag. This means that if you're traveling to a destination that is several hours ahead of your current time zone, you should try to eat meals at the appropriate times for your destination a few days before you leave. For example, if you're traveling from New York to Switzerland, which is seven hours ahead, you could start eating dinner at 9pm EST (which is 3am Switzerland time) a few days before your trip.

By adjusting your eating schedule before you travel, you can help to shift your body's clock closer to the destination's time zone, which can make it easier to adjust to the new schedule once you arrive.

Accommodation

Your two biggest expenses when travelling to Switzerland are accommodation and food. This section is intended to help you cut these costs dramatically without compromising on those luxury feels:

How to Book a Five-star Hotel consistently on the Cheap in Switzerland

The cheapest four and five-star hotel deals are available when you 'blind book'. Blind booking is a type of discounted hotel booking where the guest doesn't know the name of the hotel until after they've booked and paid for the reservation. This allows hotels to offer lower prices without damaging their brand image or cannibalizing their full-price bookings.

Here are some of the best platforms for blind booking a hotel in Switzerland:

1. Hotwire - This website offers discounted hotel rates for blind booking. You can choose the star rating, neighborhood, and amenities you want, but the actual hotel name will not be revealed until after you've booked.
2. Priceline - Once you've made the reservation, the hotel name and location will be revealed.
3. Secret Escapes - This website offers luxury hotel deals at discounted rates. You can choose the type of hotel you want and the general location, but the hotel name and exact location will be revealed after you book.
4. Lastminute.com - You can select the star rating and general location, but the hotel name and exact location will be revealed after booking. Using the Top Secret hotels you can find a four star hotel from $60 a night in Switzerland - consistently! Most of the hotels featured are in the Grange Group. If in doubt, simply copy and paste the description into Google to find the name before booking.

Off-Peak Travel:
Plan your visit during the off-peak seasons when demand is lower. This may lead to reduced room rates and special promotions.

Weekday Stays:
Hotels in Switzerland have much lower rates on weekdays compared to weekends. If your travel dates are flexible, consider staying during the week.

Book in Advance:
Take advantage of early booking discounts. Some hotels offer lower rates if you book well in advance.

Use Price Comparison Websites:
Utilize hotel booking websites and apps to compare prices across multiple platforms. Look for discounts, promotions, or exclusive deals offered by these platforms.

Join Loyalty Programs:
Sign up for the loyalty programs of hotel chains. Members often receive exclusive discounts, room upgrades, and other perks.

Bundle Packages:
Consider booking hotel and flight packages. Sometimes, bundling services can result in overall cost savings.

Look for Package Deals:
Some luxury hotels offer packages that include meals, spa services, or other amenities. These packages might provide better value than booking individual services.

Check for Special Promotions:
Monitor the hotel's official website for special promotions, seasonal sales, or limited-time offers.

Use Discount Codes:
Look for discount codes or promotional offers when booking. These codes may be available through the hotel's website, email newsletters, or third-party booking platforms.

Consider Alternative Accommodations:
Explore other luxury accommodation options such as boutique hotels, bed and breakfasts, or vacation rentals. They might offer competitive rates compared to traditional five-star hotels.

Book Last Minute:
If you are flexible with your travel dates, consider booking last-minute deals. Some hotels may offer discounted rates to fill empty rooms.

Negotiate Directly:
After finding the best rate online, contact the hotel directly to see if they can offer a better deal or provide additional perks.

Cash Back and Rewards Programs:
Use credit cards that offer cash back or rewards for hotel bookings. This can provide additional savings over time.

Enjoy the Finest Five-star Hotels for a 10th of the Cost

If you travel during the peak season or during a major event, you can still enjoy the finest hotels in Switzerland for a 10th of the normal cost. With a day pass, you can enjoy all the amenities that the hotel has to offer, including the pool, spa, gym, and included lunches at fine restaurants. This can be a great way to relax and unwind for a day without having to spend money on an overnight stay.

Here are some of the best luxury day passes Switzerland hotels:

Badrutt's Palace Hotel - St. Moritz:

Nestled in the lap of the Swiss Alps, Badrutt's Palace Hotel stands as a luxurious alpine resort, boasting unparalleled views of the surrounding landscapes. This iconic establishment offers a day pass that extends beyond mere indulgence, providing privileged access to its spa facilities and an exquisite dining experience.

The Dolder Grand - Zurich:

Exuding sophistication in every detail, The Dolder Grand in Zurich is more than just a hotel—it's an immersive retreat. With a focus on refinement, this establishment offers day passes that unlock access to its spa oasis, inviting guests to partake in the serenity of its pool and the invigoration of its fitness facilities, all complemented by the culinary excellence of its fine dining options.

Kulm Hotel - St. Moritz:

With a legacy steeped in elegance and tradition, the Kulm Hotel in St. Moritz is a testament to timeless luxury. Beyond its storied history, the hotel's day passes open the doors to a world of relaxation, providing guests with access to spa amenities and an array of other meticulously designed hotel facilities.

Bürgenstock Hotel - Lake Lucerne:

Perched above Lake Lucerne, the Bürgenstock Hotel is a sanctuary of opulence and natural beauty. Offering sweeping vistas, day passes at this retreat include access to the rejuvenating spa, a wellness area designed for tranquility, and an outdoor pool that mirrors the breathtaking surroundings.

Grand Hotel Kronenhof - Pontresina:

Immersed in the breathtaking scenery of Pontresina, the Grand Hotel Kronenhof stands as a classic Swiss haven. Beyond its picturesque setting, day passes to this historic establishment grant guests exclusive access to the spa and wellness facilities, promising a rejuvenating experience amidst the timeless charm of the Alps.

Baur au Lac - Zurich:

Situated in close proximity to the serene Lake Zurich, Baur au Lac is a luxury hotel that seamlessly blends modernity with timeless elegance. Day passes here offer access to the state-of-the-art fitness center and an indulgent spa, allowing guests to unwind in a setting that reflects the hotel's commitment to sophistication.

Victoria-Jungfrau Grand Hotel & Spa - Interlaken:

A harmonious blend of history and modern luxury, the Victoria-Jungfrau Grand Hotel & Spa in Interlaken stands as a testament to Swiss hospitality. Day passes beckon guests to experience the historic charm complemented by modern amenities, including access to the spa, fitness center, and an inviting pool.

Mont Cervin Palace - Zermatt:
Nestled in the heart of Zermatt, Mont Cervin Palace is a charming retreat that captures the essence of its surroundings. Day passes at this establishment open the doors to spa indulgence and a host of recreational facilities, promising a delightful escape amidst the captivating landscapes of Zermatt.

TOP TIP: AVOID The weekend price hike in summer

Hotel prices skyrocket during weekends in peak season (June, July, August and December). If you can, get out of Switzerland for the weekend you'll save thousands on luxury hotels. For example a room at a popular five-star hotel costs $80 a night during the week when blind-booking. That price goes to $400 a night for Saturday's and Sundays. Amazing nearby weekend trips are featured further on and planning those on the weekends could easily save you a ton of money and make your trip more comfortable by avoiding crowds.

Strategies to Book Five-Star Hotels for Two-Star Prices in Switzerland

Use Time

There are two ways to use time. One is to book in advance. Three months will net you the best deal, especially if your visit coincides with an event. The other is to book on the day of your stay. This is a risky move, but if executed well, you can lay your head in a five-star hotel for a 2-star fee.

Before you travel to Switzerland, check for big events using a simple google search 'What's on in Switzerland', if you find no big events drawing travellers, risk showing up with no accommodation booked (If there are big events on demand exceeds supply and you should avoid using this strategy). If you don't want to risk showing up with no accommodation booked, book a cheap accommodation with free-cancellation.

Before I go into demand-based pricing, take a moment to think about your risk tolerance. By risk, I am not talking about personal safety. No amount of financial savings is worth risking that. What I am talking about is being inconvenienced. Do you deal well with last-minute changes? Can you roll with the punches or do you freak out if something changes? Everyone is different and knowing yourself is the best way to plan a great trip. If you are someone that likes to have everything pre-planned using demand-based pricing to get cheap accommodation will not work for you.

Demand-based pricing

Be they an Airbnb host or hotel manager; no one wants empty rooms. Most will do anything to make some revenue because they still have the same costs to cover whether the room is occupied or not. That's why you will find many hotels drastically slashing room rates for same-day bookings.

How to book five-star hotels for a two-star price

You will not be able to find these discounts when the demand exceeds the supply. So if you're visiting during the peak season, or during an event which has drawn many travellers again don't try this.

1. On the day of your stay, visit booking.com (which offers better discounts than Kayak and agoda.com). Hotel
   Tonight individually checks for any last-minute bookings, but they take a big chunk of the action, so the better deals come from booking.com.
2. The best results come from booking between 2 pm and 4 pm when the risk of losing any revenue with no occupancy is most pronounced, so algorithms supporting hotels slash prices. This is when you can find rates that are not within the "lowest publicly visible" rate.

3. To avoid losing customers to other websites, or cheapening the image of their hotel most will only offer the super cheap rates during a two hour window from 2 pm to 4 pm. Two guests will pay 10x difference in price but it's absolutely vital to the hotel that neither knows it.

Takeaway: To get the lowest price book on the day of stay between 2 pm and 4 pm and extend your search radius to include further afield hotels with good transport connections.

There are several luxury hotels outside of Switzerland's city center that offer good transport connections to the city, as well as easy access to other nearby attractions. Here are a few options to consider:

1. The Grove: This five-star hotel is located in Hertfordshire, just 18 miles north of Switzerland. It offers a free shuttle bus to and from Watford Junction station, where you can catch a train into Switzerland's Euston station in just 18 minutes. The hotel also has its own golf course, spa, and several dining options.
2. Coworth Park: This luxurious country house hotel is located in Ascot, about 25 miles west of Switzerland. It offers easy access to Heathrow Airport, as well as direct train connections to Switzerland's Waterloo station from nearby Sunningdale station. The hotel has its own polo fields, spa, and Michelin-starred restaurant.
3. Pennyhill Park Hotel and Spa: This five-star hotel is located in Surrey, just 30 miles southwest of Switzerland. It is easily accessible by car or train, with direct connections to Switzerland's Waterloo station from nearby Bagshot station. The hotel has a large spa, several dining options, and is set on 123 acres of landscaped gardens and parkland.
4. Cliveden House: This historic country house hotel is located in Berkshire, about 25 miles west of Switzerland. It is easily accessible by car or train, with direct connections to Switzerland's Paddington station from nearby Taplow station. The hotel has a spa, several dining options, and is set on 376 acres of National Trust gardens and parkland.

These are just a few examples of luxury hotels outside of Switzerland's city center with good transport connections to the city and opportunities for last-minute discounts.

Priceline Hack to get a Luxury Hotel on the Cheap

Priceline.com has been around since 1997 and is an incredible site for sourcing luxury Hotels on the cheap in Switzerland.

Priceline have a database of the lowest price a hotel will accept for a particular time and date. That amount changes depending on two factors:

1. Demand: More demand high prices.
2. Likelihood of lost revenue: if the room is still available at 3pm the same-day prices will plummet.

Obviously they don't want you to know the lowest price as they make more commission the higher the price you pay.

They offer two good deals to entice you to book with them in Switzerland. And the good news is neither require last-minute booking (though the price will decrease the closer to the date you book).

'Firstly, 'price-breakers'. You blind book from a choice of three highly rated hotels which they name. Pricebreakers, travelers are shown three similar, highly-rated hotels, listed under a single low price.' After you book they reveal the name of the hotel.

Secondly, the 'express deals'. These are the last minute deals. You'll be able to see the name of the hotel before you book.

To find the right luxury hotel for you at a cheap price you should plug in the neighbourhoods you want to stay in, an acceptable rating (4 or 5 stars), and filter by the amenities you want.

You can also get an addition discount for your Switzerland hotel by booking on their dedicated app.

How to trick travel Algorithms to get the lowest hotel price

Do not believe anyone who says changing your IP address to get cheaper hotels or flights does NOT work. If you don't believe us, download a Tor Network and search for flights and hotels to one destination using your current IP and then the tor network (a tor browser hides your IP address from algorithms. It is commonly used by hackers). You will receive different prices.

The price you see is a decision made by an algorithm that adjusts prices using data points such as past bookings, remaining capacity, average demand and the probability of selling the room or flight later at a higher price. If knows you've searched for the area before ip the prices high. To circumvent this, you can either use a different IP address from a cafe or airport or data from an international sim. I use a sim from Three, which provides free data in many countries around the world. When you search from a new IP address, most of the time, and particularly near booking you will get a lower price. Sometimes if your sim comes from a 'rich' country, say the UK or USA, you will see higher rates as the algorithm has learnt people from these countries pay more. The solution is to book from a local wifi connection - but a different one from the one you originally searched from.

The cheapest places to stay

Bauernhof (Straw Farm Stays)

Swiss farms often offer unique experiences, including straw accommodations. Prices vary, you can find options ranging from CHF 10 to CHF 80 per person per night. These stays provide a rustic, charming atmosphere.

Farm Stay Switzerland: This website specializes in farm stays in Switzerland. You can search for Bauernhof accommodations based on location, amenities, and activities.

Campsites:

> Switzerland offers numerous campsites equipped for RVs. Prices vary depending on location and amenities. Expect to pay anywhere from CHF 20 to CHF 50 per night. Popular sites include Camping Jungfrau in Lauterbrunnen and TCS Camping in Interlaken.

Aires and Stopovers:

> Some areas have designated Aires or stopovers where RVs can park overnight. These are usually more budget-friendly but may lack facilities. Prices can range from CHF 10 to CHF 30 per night.

Stay in university dorms in Switzerland.

Prices for university dorms in Switzerland start at 30 CHF a night and many offer dorm rooms during the summer vacation. Here are the universites with the best offers, rooms are private and many include wash facilities:

- University of Zurich (UZH):
- ETH Zurich (Swiss Federal Institute of Technology):
- University of Geneva:
- University of Lausanne (UNIL):
- University of Basel:
- University of Bern:
- University of St. Gallen (HSG):

Swiss mountain huts

Swiss mountain huts, also known as "Berghütten" or "SAC huts" (managed by the Swiss Alpine Club), provide a rustic and budget-friendly accommodation option for hikers and mountaineers. These mountain huts offer a unique and scenic accommodation option. Prices can vary, but they often range from CHF 40 to CHF 100 per person per night. These huts provide basic facilities and are popular among hikers and outdoor enthusiasts.

Staying in Swiss Mountain Huts:

> **Reservations:**

Check availability and make reservations in advance, especially during peak seasons like summer and early fall. You can use the online reservation system provided by the Swiss Alpine Club (SAC).

SAC Membership:
While non-members can stay in SAC huts, members enjoy discounted rates. Consider becoming a member if you plan to stay in multiple huts during your trip.

What to Bring:
Pack lightly, as you'll need to carry your belongings. Bring a sleeping bag, personal hygiene items, and any additional necessities. Meals are often provided in the huts, but it's good to check in advance.

Accommodation Types:
Huts offer different types of accommodations, from shared dormitories to private rooms. Prices vary based on the type of accommodation.

Meals:
Many huts provide meals, and you might opt for a half-board package that includes dinner and breakfast. Alternatively, you can bring your own food, but cooking facilities may be limited.

Prices:

SAC Hut Prices:
Prices vary widely depending on the hut's location, facilities, and services. On average, you might expect to pay anywhere from CHF 30 to CHF 80 or more per person per night. SAC members usually receive a discount.

Meals:
A three-course dinner and breakfast might cost an additional CHF 20 to CHF 40.

Discounts:
SAC members often receive a discount of around CHF 10 to CHF 20 per night. If you're planning to stay in multiple huts, the membership fee can quickly pay off.

Combining these options—hostels, budget hotels, Airbnb, camping, and mountain huts—allows you to tailor your accommodation choices based on your preferences and the regions you plan to visit and also plan for weekend price hikes. You can stay in a five-star hotel on a Monday for a fraction you can stay in the same room on a Sunday!

Cheapest Areas to Stay in an Airbnb in Switzerland

While Airbnb's don't come with daily cleanings and room-service, they can be luxury. Switzerland has a diverse range of villages and towns, each with its own unique character and charm. Here are some areas that are great for cheap Airbnb stays:

Fribourg:
A charming city with medieval architecture and a relaxed atmosphere, often more affordable compared to larger Swiss cities.

Thun:
Located on the shores of Lake Thun, this town offers a beautiful setting and is relatively more affordable than some nearby tourist hotspots.

Locarno:
Situated in the Italian-speaking part of Switzerland, Locarno is known for its Mediterranean flair. Accommodations here can be more affordable, especially compared to larger cities.

Neuchâtel:
A city on the shores of Lake Neuchâtel, offering a mix of history and culture. Accommodations here may be more affordable compared to major tourist destinations.

Winterthur:
Close to Zurich but often with more budget-friendly options, Winterthur is known for its art, culture, and gardens.

Aarau:
A small town with a well-preserved old town and convenient access to larger cities. It can be a more affordable option for accommodation.

Bellinzona:
Known for its medieval castles, Bellinzona is located in the Italian-speaking canton of Ticino. Accommodations here can be relatively more affordable compared to larger cities.

Schaffhausen:
Home to the impressive Rhine Falls, Schaffhausen offers a quieter setting. Accommodations may be more affordable compared to larger cities.

Chur:
The oldest town in Switzerland, Chur offers a mix of history and natural beauty. Accommodations here may be more affordable compared to larger cities.

Brig:
A town in the Valais region with easy access to the Alps, Brig can offer more budget-friendly options compared to popular ski resorts.

How to get last-minute discounts on owner rented properties

In addition to Airbnb, you can also find owner rented rooms and apartments on www.vrbo.com or HomeAway or a host of others.

Nearly all owners renting accommodation will happily give renters a "last-minute" discount to avoid the space sitting empty, not earning a dime.

Go to Airbnb or another platform and put in today's date. Once you've found something you like start the negotiating by asking for a 25% reduction. A sample message to an Airbnb host might read:

Dear HOST NAME,

I love your apartment. It looks perfect for me. Unfortunately, I'm on a very tight budget. I hope you won't be offended, but I wanted to ask if you would be amenable to offering me a 25% discount for tonight, tomorrow and the following day? I see that you aren't booked. I can assure you, I will leave your place exactly the way I found it. I will put bed linen in the washer and ensure everything is clean for the next guest. I would be delighted to bring you a bottle of wine to thank you for any discount that you could offer.

If this sounds okay, please send me a custom offer, and I will book straight away.

YOUR NAME.

In my experience, a polite, genuine message like this, that proposes reciprocity will be successful 80% of the time. Don't ask for more than 25% off, this person still has to pay the bills and will probably say no as your stay will cost them more in bills than they make. Plus starting higher, can offend the owner and do you want to stay somewhere, where you have offended the host?

In Practice

To use either of these methods, you must travel light. Less stuff means greater mobility, everything is faster and you don't have to check-in or store luggage. If you have a lot of luggage, you're going to have fewer of these opportunities to save on accommodation. Plus travelling light benefits the planet - you're buying, consuming, and transporting less stuff.

Blind-booking

If your risk tolerance does not allow for last-minute booking, you can use blind-booking. Many hotels not wanting to cheapen their brand with known low-prices, choose to operate a blind booking policy. This is where you book without knowing the name of the hotel you're going to stay in until you've made the payment. This is also sometimes used as a marketing strategy where the hotel is seeking to recover from past issues. I've stayed in plenty of blind book hotels. As long as you choose 4 or 5 star hotels, you will find them to be clean, comfortable and safe. priceline.com, Hot Rate® Hotels and Top Secret Hotels (operated by lastminute.com) offer the best deals.

Hotels.com Loyalty Program

This is currently the best hotel loyalty program with hotels in Switzerland. The basic premise is you collect 10 nights and get 1 free. hotels.com price match, so if booking.com has a cheaper price you can get hotel.com, to match. If you intend to travel more than ten nights in a year, its a great choice to get the 11th free.

Don't let time use you.
Rigidity will cost you money. You pay the price you're willing to pay, not the amount it requires a hotel to deliver. Therefore if you're in town for a big event, saving money on accommodation is nearly impossible so in such cases book three months ahead.

How to trick travel Algorithms to get the lowest hotel price

Do not believe anyone who says changing your IP address to get cheaper hotels or flights does NOT work. If you don't believe us, download a Tor Network and search for flights and hotels to one destination using your current IP and then the tor network (a tor browser hides your IP address from algorithms. It is commonly used by hackers). You will receive different prices.

The price you see is a decision made by an algorithm that adjusts prices using data points such as past bookings, remaining capacity, average demand and the probability of selling the room or flight later at a higher price. If knows you've searched for the area before ip the prices high. To circumvent this, you can either use a different IP address from a cafe or airport or data from an international sim. I use a sim from Three, which provides free data in many countries around the world. When you search from a new IP address, most of the time, and particularly near booking you will get a lower price. Sometimes if your sim comes from a 'rich' country, say the UK or USA, you will see higher rates as the algorithm has learnt people from these countries pay more. The solution is to book from a local wifi connection - but a different one from the one you originally searched from.

Saving Money on Food

If you walk-in to any Switzerland restaurant without planning you can easily walk out with a bill for 50 euros plus per person, so it pays to know how to eat well cheaply.

The high cost of food in Switzerland can be attributed to several factors, including the country's consistently high cost of living, stringent quality standards, geographical challenges such as mountainous terrain and a landlocked location necessitating significant food imports, and relatively high labor costs. As a result, everyday food items in Switzerland are notably more expensive compared to many other countries. For instance, bread (500g) can range from CHF 2.50 to CHF 4.00, milk (1 liter) from CHF 1.50 to CHF 2.50, and chicken breast (1kg) from CHF 25.00 to CHF 35.00. The emphasis on quality, fresh ingredients, and the overall high standard of living contribute to the elevated prices observed in the Swiss food market. There are several strategies to save money on food while still enjoying the local cuisine:

Apéro Time:

Instead of having a full dinner at a restaurant, consider participating in the Swiss tradition of "apéro." Enjoy a drink and some snacks during this pre-dinner social time. Here are a few suggestions:

Zurich:

- Kronenhalle: Known for its art-filled ambiance, Kronenhalle in Zurich is a classic choice for an apéro.
- Jules Verne Panorama Bar: Offers a panoramic view of Zurich and is known for its creative cocktails.

Geneva:

- Rooftop 42: Located in the heart of Geneva, it offers a stylish rooftop setting for apéritif with views of the city.
- Café du Centre: A classic Swiss brasserie with a cozy atmosphere.

Bern:

- Sky Terrace: Located at the Kursaal Bern, the Sky Terrace offers stunning views of the old town and the Alps.
- Zunft zu Webern: A historic guild house with a traditional setting.

Basel:

- Consum: A trendy bar and restaurant known for its creative drinks and international atmosphere.
- Noohn: A stylish lounge and bar with a diverse menu of cocktails and small bites.

Lausanne:

- La Brasserie de Montbenon: Offers a beautiful terrace and a relaxed atmosphere.
- Eat Me: A cocktail bar and restaurant known for its innovative drinks and tapas-style dishes.

Explore Local Bakeries:

Bakeries often offer a variety of affordable and delicious pastries and sandwiches. Grabbing breakfast or a snack from a bakery can be more budget-friendly.

BYOB (Bring Your Own Bottle):

If you choose to dine out, consider restaurants that allow you to bring your own bottle of wine to save on beverage costs.

Use Dining Apps:

Check for restaurant deals and discounts using dining apps or loyalty programs that offer rewards for frequent customers. Here are some options:

Groupon:

Groupon offers various deals, including discounts on restaurants, cafes, and other dining experiences in Switzerland.

TheFork (formerly Bookatable):

TheFork is a restaurant reservation platform that often offers special deals and discounts on dining in Switzerland. Users can make reservations and benefit from promotional offers.

Dine4less:

Dine4less provides discounts at participating restaurants in Switzerland. Users can purchase dining cards that offer a percentage off the total bill or specific dishes.

Züri wie neu:

Züri wie neu is a Zurich-based app that provides discounts and promotions for various services, including dining, entertainment, and more.

HappyCow:

HappyCow is a useful app for those looking for vegetarian, vegan, or healthy dining options. It lists restaurants, cafes, and grocery stores, and often includes user reviews.

Lokalhelden:

Lokalhelden is a Swiss app that focuses on promoting local businesses, including restaurants. It may feature special offers and discounts from local establishments.

Eat.ch:

Eat.ch is a food delivery platform in Switzerland that sometimes offers promotions and discounts for online orders. While it's more delivery-focused, it's worth checking for special deals.

Swiss Coupon Pass - 49 CHF

The Swiss Coupon Pass offers a variety of discount vouchers for dining, activities, and attractions throughout Switzerland. It's either physical pass or can be accessed digitally.

Use 'Too Good To Go'

Switzerland offers plenty of food bargains; if you know where to look. Thankfully the app 'Too Good to Go' is turning visitors into locals by showing them exactly where to find the tastiest deals. In Switzerland you can pick up a $15 buy of baked goods for $2.99. You'll also find lots of fish and meat dishes on offer in Switzerland from notable restaurants, which would normally be expensive.

How it works? You pay for a magic bag on the app and simply pick it up from the bakery or restaurant during the time they've selected. You can find extremely cheap breakfast, lunch, dinner and even groceries this way. Simply download the app and press 'my current location' to find the deals near you in Switzerland. .What's not to love about driving down food waste?

An oft-quoted parable is 'There is no such thing as cheap food. Either you pay at the cash registry or the doctor's office'. This dismisses the fact that good nutrition is a choice; we all make every-time we eat. Cheap eats are not confined to hotdogs and kebabs. The great thing about using Too Good To Go is you can eat nutritious food cheaply: fruits, vegetables, fish and nut dishes are a fraction of their supermarket cost.

Japan has the longest life expectancy in the world. A national study by the Japanese Ministry of Internal Affairs and Communications revealed that between January and May 2019, a household of two spent on average ¥65,994 a month, that's $10 per person per day on food. You truly don't need to spend a lot to eat nutritious food. That's a marketing gimmick hawkers of overpriced muesli bars want you to believe.

Opt for prix-fixe lunch menus

You'll see them all over the city. Humphrey's Switzerland has three courses for under €20.

Use delivery services on the cheap.
Take advantage of local offers on food delivery services. Most platforms including Uber Eats and Just Eat offer $10 off the first order in Switzerland.

The Cheapest Supermarket in Switzerland

Migros and Coop are two of the largest supermarket chains, and they often have a wide range of products. Denner is known for its focus on discount prices. Aldi and Lidl are also discount supermarket chains that operate in Switzerland.

Cheapest Take Away Coffee Switzerland

chains like Migros and Coop may have coffee stands where you can purchase take-away coffee at a relatively lower cost compared to specialty coffee shops.

IKEA

Ikea offers free coffee (with a FAMILY CARD).

IKEA Zurich-Brunau:
Location: Birmensdorferstrasse 317, 8055 Zürich
This IKEA store is situated in Zurich and is one of the larger locations in Switzerland. It offers a wide range of furniture, home goods, and a restaurant.
IKEA Geneva:
Location: Route de Vernier, 1214 Vernier
The IKEA store in Geneva is known for its convenient location and is a popular choice for residents in the Geneva area.
IKEA Lausanne:
Location: Avenue des Morgines 12, 1213 Petit-Lancy
The Lausanne store serves the French-speaking region of Switzerland and is known for its accessibility.
IKEA Dietlikon:
Location: Freihofstrasse 11, 8305 Dietlikon
Situated near Zurich, the Dietlikon store is another option for those in the Zurich area.

Switzerland Food Culture

Swiss cuisine is so much more than just fondue and chocolate, although those are undoubtedly delightful indulgences. To truly savor the richness of Swiss gastronomy, make sure to venture beyond the familiar and explore the diverse tapestry of regional dishes. Switzerland's food culture is a delightful blend of influences from its geography, history, and the coexistence of multiple linguistic and cultural regions.

Cheese Delights:

Switzerland is a cheese lover's paradise, and the iconic dishes of fondue and raclette are a testament to that. Imagine dipping chunks of bread into a bubbling pot of melted cheese with fondue or savoring the delightful experience of scraping melted cheese over boiled potatoes in the case of raclette.

Chocolate Bliss:

While Swiss chocolate is renowned worldwide, with Lindt, Toblerone, and Nestlé leading the way, there's so much more to discover. Treat yourself to a variety of chocolates and make sure to bring some back as a delicious souvenir.

Bread, Pastries, and More:

Swiss bakeries offer a delightful array of bread, pastries, and baked goods. Don't miss out on local specialties like "Zürcher Geschnetzeltes," a dish of sliced meat in a creamy mushroom sauce, often served alongside the crispy goodness of Rösti.

Meaty Delights:

From sausages and veal to game meats, Swiss cuisine boasts a variety of hearty meat dishes. Dive into the flavors of traditional dishes like "Zürcher Eintopf," a meat and vegetable stew, or savor the popular Swiss sausage, "Cervelat," especially during barbecues.

Regional Wonders:

Switzerland's cultural diversity is reflected in its culinary offerings. Each linguistic region, be it German, French, Italian, or Romansh-speaking, has its own culinary specialties. Explore "Fondue Savoyarde" in the French-speaking part or savor Italian-inspired cuisine in the Ticino region.

Seasonal and Local Embrace:

Swiss cuisine celebrates the freshness of seasonal and local ingredients. The bounty from local farms contributes to the authenticity and quality of Swiss dishes.

Alpine Comforts:

The influence of the Swiss Alps is evident in hearty dishes like "Älplermagronen," a comforting pasta and cheese dish often accompanied by applesauce.

Dining Etiquette:
In Swiss dining culture, punctuality is valued, and arriving on time for meals is customary. Sharing meals with friends and family is a cherished social activity. Embrace local customs, such as saying "bon appétit" in French-speaking areas or "en guete" in German-speaking regions, as it adds a touch of politeness to your culinary adventures.

How to get breakfast for under $5 in Switzerland

- **Local Bakeries and Cafés:** Look for local bakeries or small cafés, especially in non-touristy areas. They might offer affordable pastries, sandwiches, or coffee.
- **Supermarkets and Grocery Stores:** Purchase items for a simple breakfast from supermarkets or grocery stores. Bread, cheese, yogurt, and fruit are usually available at reasonable prices.
- **Takeaway Options:** Opt for takeaway options rather than sitting down in a restaurant. This can help save on service charges.
- **Hotel Options:** If your accommodation includes breakfast, take advantage of it. Many hotels offer a complimentary or reasonably priced breakfast buffet.
- **Food Markets:** Visit local food markets where you might find fresh produce and snacks that can make for a cost-effective breakfast.

Best Food Trucks and Street Foods

Switzerland may not be as renowned for street food as some other countries, but you can still find interesting offerings from food trucks and street vendors. Here are a few to consider:

- **Raclette Sandwiches:**
  - *Description:* Experience the Swiss love for melted cheese with Raclette sandwiches. Melted Raclette cheese is scraped onto bread, often accompanied by pickles or other toppings.
  - *Where to Find:* Look for local street vendors or markets offering this cheesy delight.
- **Älplermagronen:**
  - *Description:* A hearty Swiss dish consisting of pasta, potatoes, cheese, and onions. It's a comforting and filling option, perfect for a quick street food meal.

- *Where to Find:* Some food trucks and markets may serve Älplermagronen during colder months.
- **Zürcher Geschnetzeltes:**
  - *Description:* Sliced veal in a creamy mushroom sauce, often served with Rösti (Swiss-style grated and fried potatoes). While it's more of a traditional dish, some vendors may offer portable versions.
  - *Where to Find:* Seek out local markets or events for variations of this classic Swiss dish.
- **Gelato and Swiss Chocolate:**
  - *Description:* While not exclusive to Switzerland, the country boasts excellent gelato and chocolate. Street vendors or small gelaterias often provide high-quality treats.
  - *Where to Find:* Look for gelato stands in tourist areas or chocolatiers offering on-the-go options.
- **Saffron Risotto Balls (Risotto Supplì):**
  - *Description:* Inspired by Italian arancini, these risotto balls are often filled with saffron-infused rice and cheese, then deep-fried to perfection.
  - *Where to Find:* Some street food events or food trucks may offer creative variations of risotto balls.

Unique desserts

Switzerland is known for its delicious and diverse desserts, many of which have interesting histories. Here are a few unique Swiss desserts along with their backgrounds:

- **Meringues:**
  - *History:* Meringues are a popular Swiss dessert made from whipped egg whites and sugar. The town of Meiringen claims to be the birthplace of meringues, with a story dating back to the 17th century. Legend has it that a pastry chef created these sweet treats by accident when he forgot a bowl of whipped egg whites in the oven overnight.
- **Nusstorte (Nut Tart):**
  - *History:* Originating from the Engadin region, Nusstorte is a rich and nut-filled tart. It's believed that the recipe dates back to the 19th century and was influenced by Turkish and Italian baking traditions. The dessert became popular in the canton of Graubünden.
- **Zuger Kirschtorte (Zug Cherry Cake):**
  - *History:* Zuger Kirschtorte is a layered cake made with sponge cake, buttercream, and cherry liqueur (Kirschwasser). Created in the town of Zug, it's said that a Zug pastry chef invented the cake in 1921, inspired by the traditional Black Forest Cake.
- **Engadiner Nusstorte (Engadin Nut Cake):**
  - *History:* This caramelized nut-filled tart is a specialty of the Engadin valley. The recipe is believed to have been brought to the region by bakers from Italy. The layers of the tart symbolize the different social classes in the Engadin, with the nut filling representing the wealthy and the crust symbolizing the less affluent.
- **Aargauer Rüeblitorte (Aargau Carrot Cake):**

- *History:* Aargauer Rüeblitorte is a carrot cake originating from the Aargau region. It is said to have been created in the early 20th century when sugar beet farmers sought new uses for their crop. The cake gained popularity for its moist texture and sweet flavor.

Must try cheap eats in each city in Switzerland

Switzerland offers a variety of delicious eats, and while some places might be on the pricier side, you can find affordable and tasty options. Here are must-try cheap eats in different cities along with tips on where to find them:

- **Zurich: Bratwurst**
    - **Where to Eat:** Head to Zeughauskeller or Sternen Grill for a classic Swiss bratwurst experience. These places are known for serving high-quality sausages.
- **Geneva: Quiches and Pastries**
    - **Where to Eat:** Visit local bakeries such as Boulangerie Poilâne or Stettler Patisserie for delicious quiches and pastries.
- **Bern: Rösti**
    - **Where to Eat:** Try rösti, a Swiss potato dish, at Bern's iconic Zunfthaus zu Metzgern or Kornhauskeller. These venues offer a cozy atmosphere to enjoy this Swiss specialty.
- **Lucerne: Älplermagronen**
    - **Where to Eat:** Sample Älplermagronen, a Swiss macaroni and cheese dish, at Rathaus Brauerei or Fritschi Restaurant. These places provide a taste of traditional Swiss comfort food.
- **Basel: Basler Läckerli**
    - **Where to Eat:** For the famous Basler Läckerli, visit Confiserie Schiesser or Läckerli Huus. These shops are known for their quality and authenticity.
- **Lausanne: Crêpes**
    - **Where to Eat:** Explore the crêperies in Lausanne, such as Crêperie d'Ouchy or Le Saint-Laurent. These spots offer a variety of sweet and savory crêpes at reasonable prices.
- **St. Moritz: Maluns**
    - **Where to Eat:** Try Maluns, a Graubünden dish, at local restaurants like Chesa Veglia or Hanselmann. These establishments offer a taste of regional specialties.
- **Interlaken: Swiss Chocolate**
    - **Where to Eat:** While not a traditional meal, indulge in Swiss chocolate at shops like Läderach or Funky Chocolate Club. It's a sweet treat to enjoy while exploring Interlaken.
- **Lugano: Risotto**
    - **Where to Eat:** Savor a plate of delicious risotto at Ristorante Toscano or Grotto Morchino. These restaurants showcase the Italian influence in the region.
- **Zermatt: Fondue**
    - **Where to Eat:** Enjoy a cozy fondue experience at places like Walliserstube or Restaurant Du Pont. These venues offer a warm and inviting atmosphere for indulging in this classic Swiss dish.

How to experience your first day in Switzerland for under $50

Experiencing your first day in Switzerland on a budget requires some strategic planning. Here's a budget-friendly itinerary to make the most of your day for under $50:

- **Breakfast at a Bakery or Café:**
    - Start your day with a simple yet satisfying breakfast from a local bakery or café. Grab a croissant, pastry, or a sandwich along with a coffee. Budget: $10-15.
- **Explore the Old Town or Free Attractions:**
    - Wander through the charming Old Town of the city you're in. Many Swiss cities have picturesque old quarters with narrow streets and historic buildings. Explore the area, take photos, and enjoy the atmosphere. Opt for free attractions like city parks or viewpoints. Budget: $0.
- **Lunch at a Grocery Store or Food Market:**
    - Save money on lunch by buying fresh produce, sandwiches, or salads from a grocery store or food market. Enjoy a picnic in a local park or by the lakeside. Budget: $10-15.
- **Free City Walking Tour:**
    - Join a free walking tour to learn about the city's history and landmarks. Many cities offer these tours, and you can tip the guide based on your budget. It's a great way to get oriented and discover interesting facts. Budget: $5-10 (tip).
- **Visit a Museum on Free Days or Discounted Hours:**
    - Check if any museums offer free entry on certain days or discounted rates during specific hours. This is a cost-effective way to experience Swiss culture and history. Budget: $10-15.
- **Relax by a Lake or River:**
    - Switzerland is known for its stunning lakes and rivers. Spend some time relaxing by the water, enjoying the scenery. It's a free and serene way to experience the beauty of the country. Budget: $0.
- **Dinner at a Takeaway or Budget-Friendly Restaurant:**
    - For dinner, opt for a takeaway meal or dine in a budget-friendly restaurant. Look for local eateries serving affordable Swiss or international cuisine. Budget: $15-20.
- **Free Evening Entertainment:**
    - Check if there are any free events or street performances happening in the evening. Some cities host free concerts, art exhibitions, or cultural events. Enjoy the local entertainment without spending extra money. Budget: $0.

Total Estimated Budget: $50 (approximate and may vary based on location and personal preferences).

Swiss Travel Pass

Product	Price in CHF in 2nd class	Price in CHF in 1st class
Swiss Travel Pass 3 days	232.–	369.–
Swiss Travel Pass 4 days	281.–	447.–
Swiss Travel Pass 6 days	359.–	570.–
Swiss Travel Pass 8 days	389.–	617.–
Swiss Travel Pass 15 days	429.–	675.–

This all-in-one pass provides unlimited travel on the extensive and efficient Swiss Travel System network, encompassing trains, buses, and boats. With the pass, you have the flexibility to hop on and off public transportation at your convenience, allowing seamless exploration of Switzerland's picturesque landscapes and charming cities. Additionally, the Swiss Travel Pass grants free or discounted entry to numerous museums and attractions, offering a cultural immersion into the rich history and heritage of the country. The convenience of not needing to purchase individual tickets for each journey and the potential for substantial cost savings, especially for those planning an itinerary with multiple stops, make the Swiss Travel Pass an invaluable companion for an immersive and budget-friendly Swiss travel experience.

It's a consecutive-day pass, so you've got to map out your itinerary carefully to make sure you're getting your money's worth.

To maximize the value of your Swiss train pass, use these tips:

- **Regional Trains:** Use regional trains instead of high-speed ones, as they are often covered by the pass and can provide scenic routes.
- **Free Boat and Bus Rides:** Some Swiss passes include boat and bus rides. Take advantage of these options to explore different areas without extra cost.
- **Discounted Attractions:** Swiss passes often offer discounts on museums, cable cars, and other attractions. Check for partner offers and save on entrance fees.
- **Flexible Pass Duration:** Choose a pass duration that aligns with your travel plans. If you're staying for a week, a 7-day pass might be more cost-effective than individual tickets.
- **Children and Family Passes:** If you're traveling with family, consider family passes or discounted child tickets to save on overall costs.
- **Book in Advance:** Some scenic trains require reservations. Book these in advance to secure your seat and potentially benefit from lower fares.
- **Use the Pass for City Transportation:** In some Swiss cities, the pass covers local transportation. Utilize this feature to explore city attractions at no additional cost.
- **Explore Less Touristy Areas:** Venture off the beaten path to smaller towns and villages where your pass can still be valuable, and you can experience authentic Swiss culture.

Optimize your Swiss itinerary

Swiss Train tickets start at 50 CHF. These costs can really add up so make sure you optimize your routes. Here is a logical order and grouping of destinations to minimize unnecessary travel:

- **Zurich:**
    - Start your journey in Zurich, explore the city's vibrant culture, and visit key attractions like the Old Town and Lake Zurich.
- **Lucerne:**
    - Head to Lucerne, a short train ride from Zurich. Enjoy the picturesque Old Town, Chapel Bridge, and take a boat trip on Lake Lucerne.
- **Interlaken:**
    - Travel to Interlaken, nestled between Lake Thun and Lake Brienz. Use it as a base for exploring the Jungfrau region and enjoy activities like hiking or taking the Jungfraujoch train.
- **Lauterbrunnen Valley:**
    - Explore Lauterbrunnen Valley, known for its stunning waterfalls. Visit Trümmelbach Falls and take the cable car to Mürren for breathtaking views.
- **Grindelwald:**
    - Move to Grindelwald, another charming mountain village. Experience the First Flyer or hike the Eiger Trail for panoramic views.
- **Zermatt:**
    - Travel to Zermatt, famous for the iconic Matterhorn. Explore the car-free village and consider taking the Gornergrat Railway for stunning vistas.
- **Montreux:**

- Head to Montreux, located on Lake Geneva. Enjoy the lakeside promenade and consider a visit to Chillon Castle.
- **Geneva:**
  - Finish your journey in Geneva, exploring international organizations, the Jet d'Eau, and the United Nations headquarters.

By following this itinerary, you'll cover diverse landscapes, experience both cities and mountain villages, and minimize unnecessary backtracking. Adjust the duration at each location based on your interests and travel pace. Additionally, use the Swiss Travel Pass for seamless travel between destinations.

Another thing to keep in mind is that while the pass covers a good chunk of the Swiss Travel System, it might not be your golden ticket to every mountain railway or cable car in the Alps. If you're dreaming of those iconic mountain excursions, you might need to grab a separate ticket. And speaking of tickets, the pass doesn't roll out the red carpet for premium trains like the Glacier Express or Bernina Express—those will cost you extra.

If you're more of a spontaneous, here-and-there traveler, you might need to explore other options. Despite these quirks, the Swiss Travel Pass remains a huge money saving travel companion for many, so just weigh your options and plan accordingly for your needs and desires.

To maximize your savings, it's essential to plan your itinerary efficiently. Here's a suggested itinerary for a 7-day trip:

7-Day Itinerary

Day 1: Arrival in Zurich

- Arrive in Zurich and activate your Swiss Travel Pass after you recover from jet lag.
- Explore Zurich using public transportation.
- Visit free museums like the Swiss National Museum or Kunsthaus Zurich.

Day 2: Lucerne Day Trip

- Take a train to Lucerne.
- Enjoy a boat cruise on Lake Lucerne (included in the pass).
- Explore the old town, Chapel Bridge, Water Tower, and the Lion Monument.
- Return to Zurich in the evening.

Day 3: Interlaken and Lauterbrunnen

- Take a train to Interlaken.
- Explore the town and take a boat trip on Lake Thun or Lake Brienz.
- In the afternoon, visit Lauterbrunnen and Trümmelbach Falls.
- Return to Zurich or stay overnight in Interlaken.

Day 4: Day Trip to Jungfraujoch

- Take a train from Interlaken to Jungfraujoch (Top of Europe).
- Enjoy the breathtaking views and activities at Jungfraujoch.
- Return to Interlaken or Zurich in the evening.

Day 5: Day Trip to Zermatt

- Travel to Zermatt by train.
- Explore the car-free village and take the Gornergrat Railway for stunning views.
- Visit the famous Matterhorn.
- Return to Zurich in the evening.

Day 6: Day Trip to Bern

- Take a train to Bern.
- Explore the UNESCO World Heritage-listed Old Town.
- Visit the Federal Palace and the Zentrum Paul Klee.
- Return to Zurich in the evening.

Day 7: Day Trip to Geneva

- Take a train to Geneva.
- Explore the United Nations headquarters, Jet d'Eau, and the Old Town.
- Visit free museums like the Museum of Art and History.
- Return to Zurich in the evening.

10-Day Itinerary:

Day 8-10: Explore Swiss Countryside and Additional Cities

- Use the additional days to explore more of the Swiss countryside or visit cities like Basel, Lausanne, or the Rhine Falls.
- Consider taking scenic train routes, such as the Glacier Express or Bernina Express.

Supersaver Tickets

Swiss Railways offers Supersaver Tickets, are discounted tickets available for specific trains and routes. These tickets are limited, so it's advisable to book them early. If the swiss train pass is not for you, book your trips using the supersaver tickets before you travel. Go to the official website of the Swiss Federal Railways (SBB).

Itinerary for 7 days

Experiencing a luxurious trip to Switzerland on a budget requires careful planning and prioritizing. Here's a suggested itinerary for a week, combining some high-end experiences with cost-effective choices:

Day 1: Zurich

- *Morning:* Arrive in Zurich and start your day with a leisurely breakfast at a Brezelkönig café.
- *Afternoon:* Explore the Old Town (Altstadt) and visit free attractions like Grossmünster and Lindenhof.
- *Evening:* Enjoy a luxurious dinner at a mid-range Swiss restaurant in the Old Town.

Day 2: Lucerne

- *Morning:* Take a scenic train to Lucerne and have breakfast at a local bakery.
- *Afternoon:* Explore Chapel Bridge, Water Tower, and Old Town. Visit the Richard Wagner Museum (free entry).
- *Evening:* Splurge on a Swiss fondue dinner at a reputable restaurant by the lake.

Day 3: Interlaken

- *Morning:* Travel to Interlaken and start the day with a hearty breakfast.
- *Afternoon:* Explore the town and take a leisurely stroll along Höheweg.
- *Evening:* Opt for a cable car ride to Harder Kulm for sunset views. Have a reasonably priced dinner in the town.

Day 4: Lauterbrunnen Valley

- *Morning:* Visit Trümmelbach Falls and have breakfast in Lauterbrunnen.
- *Afternoon:* Hike or take a train to Wengen for stunning views of the Alps.
- *Evening:* Enjoy dinner at a cozy mountain restaurant with local specialties.

Day 5: Zermatt

- *Morning:* Take a train to Zermatt and have breakfast with a view of the Matterhorn.
- *Afternoon:* Explore the car-free village and enjoy a cable car ride or hike.
- *Evening:* Have a gourmet dinner at a mid-range restaurant with Swiss cuisine.

Day 6: Geneva

- *Morning:* Travel to Geneva and start your day with a lakeside breakfast.
- *Afternoon:* Visit the Jet d'Eau and explore the United Nations area (free entry).
- *Evening:* Enjoy dinner at a local bistro or brasserie near the Old Town.

Day 7: Lausanne

- *Morning:* Visit the Olympic Museum (check for discounted entry).
- *Afternoon:* Stroll along the Ouchy Promenade and enjoy lunch by Lake Geneva.
- *Evening:* Explore the Lausanne Cathedral and have a farewell dinner at a charming restaurant.

Budget Tips:

- Utilize Swiss Travel Pass for train travel.
- Look for lunch specials and set menus for cost-effective dining.
- Consider Airbnb or budget-friendly accommodations.
- Take advantage of free attractions and enjoy the natural beauty Switzerland offers.

Remember to check for any seasonal discounts, city passes, or group rates that might enhance your budget-friendly luxury experience.

Itinerary for One Month

Planning a month-long trip to Switzerland with a luxury-on-a-budget approach requires careful consideration of expenses. Here's a suggested itinerary that balances high-end experiences with cost-effective choices:

Week 1: Zurich and Surroundings

- **Days 1-3:** Begin in Zurich, exploring the Old Town, Bahnhofstrasse, and Lake Zurich. Stay in a well-located mid-range hotel or consider Airbnb.
- **Days 4-7:** Take day trips to Rhine Falls, Lucerne, and Rigi. Explore the Swiss countryside while keeping accommodation costs in check.

Week 2: Interlaken and Jungfrau Region

- **Days 8-10:** Travel to Interlaken and enjoy the scenic beauty. Stay in a comfortable guesthouse or budget hotel.
- **Days 11-14:** Explore Lauterbrunnen Valley, Grindelwald, and Mürren. Take advantage of hiking trails and affordable local restaurants.

Week 3: Zermatt and Matterhorn

- **Days 15-18:** Head to Zermatt and marvel at the Matterhorn. Opt for budget accommodation options like mountain huts or guesthouses.
- **Days 19-21:** Enjoy Gornergrat and Klein Matterhorn. Consider a mid-range hotel or explore more budget-friendly lodging in nearby towns.

Week 4: Geneva, Lausanne, and Montreux

- **Days 22-24:** Travel to Geneva and stay in a centrally located hotel or budget-friendly accommodation.
- **Days 25-27:** Explore Lausanne and Montreux, taking advantage of the beautiful Lake Geneva region. Consider an Airbnb for a local experience.
- **Days 28-30:** Relax in Montreux and explore nearby vineyards. Indulge in local cuisine at affordable restaurants with a touch of Swiss luxury.

Budget Tips:

- **Swiss Travel Pass:** Invest in a Swiss Travel Pass for unlimited train and bus travel.
- **Accommodation:** Mix luxury stays with budget-friendly options like guesthouses, hostels, or Airbnb.
- **Meals:** Opt for lunch specials, local markets, and supermarkets for some meals.
- **Attractions:** Look for city passes or bundled tickets for attractions to save money.
- **Off-Peak Travel:** Consider traveling during the shoulder season for better rates on accommodations and fewer crowds.

Remember to book accommodations and transportation well in advance for better rates, and keep an eye out for discounts or special offers during your stay.

Snapshot: How to have a $10,000 Trip to Switzerland for $1,000 (7 days)

Category	Allocation	Breakdown	Luxury-on-a-Budget Strategy
Accommodation	$200	Five-star day passes. Mountain hut stays. Straw stays, Hostels, boutique hotels, or Airbnbs	Mix luxury stays with budget options. Use platforms like Airbnb, consider boutique hotels, or book incredible and cheap SAC huts!
Transport	$250	Trains, and public transportation	Invest in a Swiss Travel Pass for unlimited train, bus, and boat travel. or Book train or bus tickets in advance for lower prices. Consider regional travel passes for specific areas.
Food	$250	Too Good to Go. Grocery shopping, inexpensive restaurants, and street food	Opt for too good to go bags, lunch specials, local markets, and supermarkets for some meals. Explore affordable local eateries for authentic Swiss cuisine.
Activities	$150	Free or low-cost attractions, hiking, and exploring	Look for city passes or bundled tickets for attractions. Take advantage of free-entry days or discounted hours at museums and landmarks. Participate in free walking tours for city exploration or download apps for free guided hikes.
other	$150	Miscellaneous expenses like travel insurance, SIM card, and toiletries	Migros and Lidl are your money savers.
	$1,000		

Unique bargains we love in Switzerland

While Switzerland is known for its high living costs, there are numerous opportunities to enjoy the country without spending a fortune. Here are our favourites:

Free City Tours: Many Swiss cities, including Zurich, Geneva, and Basel, offer free walking tours led by locals. It's a great way to explore the city's history, architecture, and hidden gems.

Hiking and Nature Trails: Switzerland is a paradise for nature lovers. Explore the numerous hiking and nature trails for free, such as the beautiful Five Lakes Walk in Zermatt or the scenic Schynige Platte in the Bernese Oberland.

Public Art and Sculptures: Many Swiss cities have public art installations and sculptures. Stroll through city squares and parks to discover unique and often interactive art pieces.

Lakeside Relaxation: Switzerland is dotted with picturesque lakes. Enjoy a day of lakeside relaxation, whether it's Lake Geneva, Lake Lucerne, or Lake Zurich. Pack a picnic, take a swim, or simply enjoy the views.

Free City Panoramas: Instead of paying for expensive viewpoints, discover free spots that offer stunning city panoramas. In Zurich, climb to Lindenhof for a great view of the Old Town, or visit Üetliberg for a panoramic view of the city and the Alps.

Botanical Gardens: Explore the botanical gardens in various cities, such as the Botanical Garden of the University of Zurich or the Botanical Garden of Geneva. These gardens often have free entry and are perfect for a leisurely stroll.

Free Outdoor Concerts: During the summer months, many cities host free outdoor concerts and music festivals.

OUR SUPER CHEAP TIPS...

Here are our specific super cheap tips for enjoying a $10,000 trip to Switzerland for just $1,000.

Arriving

Here are the major international airports in Switzerland and how to get from them to the city:

Zurich Airport (ZRH):

- **Train:**
  Price: Approximately 6.80 CHF for a 2nd class one-way ticket.
  Details: The train station is directly below the airport, and trains run regularly to Zurich Hauptbahnhof (main station). The journey takes about 10-15 minutes.
  Tram:
  Price: Approximately 4.40 CHF for a 2nd class one-way ticket.
  Details: Tram line 10 and 12 operate between the airport and the city center. The journey takes around 30 minutes.
  Bus:
  Price: Approximately 4.40 CHF for a 2nd class one-way ticket.
  Details: Bus lines 334, 335, and 759 connect the airport to various parts of Zurich. The journey time varies depending on the specific bus route.
  Airport Shuttle Services:
  Price: Varies; can range from 20 CHF to 40 CHF or more.
  Details: Shared or private airport shuttle services are available. Prices depend on the service provider, and advance booking may offer discounts.
  Taxi:
  Price: Around 70-90 CHF, depending on traffic and exact destination.
  Details: Taxis are available at the airport, and the journey time is approximately 15-20 minutes, depending on traffic conditions.

Geneva Airport (GVA):

Here are several cost-effective transportation options from Geneva Airport (GVA) to the city center, along with estimated prices:

- **Train:**
  - **Price:** Approximately 3.10 CHF for a 2nd class one-way ticket.
  - **Details:** The train station is located within the airport, and trains run regularly to Geneva Cornavin (main station). The journey takes around 7 minutes.
- **Bus:**

- **Price:** Approximately 3 CHF for a one-way ticket.
- **Details:** Public buses (Line 5) operate from the airport to the city center. The journey takes approximately 20-30 minutes.
- **Airport Shuttle Services:**
    - **Price:** Varies; can range from 20 CHF to 40 CHF or more.
    - **Details:** Shared or private airport shuttle services are available, and prices depend on the service provider. Advance booking may offer discounts.
- **Taxi:**
    - **Price:** Around 35-45 CHF, depending on traffic and exact destination.
    - **Details:** Taxis are available at the airport, and the journey time is approximately 20 minutes, depending on traffic conditions.
- **Uber:**
    - **Price:** Varies; can be competitive with taxi prices.
    - **Details:** Uber operates in Geneva, and prices are influenced by demand and availability. The app provides real-time fare estimates.

Basel-Mulhouse Airport (BSL/MLH):

- Bus:
    - **Price:** Approximately 4 CHF for a one-way ticket.
    - **Details:** Public buses (Line 50) operate from the airport to the Basel SBB train station. The journey takes approximately 20-30 minutes.
- **Airport Shuttle Services:**
    - **Price:** Varies; can range from 20 CHF to 40 CHF or more.
    - **Details:** Shared or private airport shuttle services are available, and prices depend on the service provider. Advance booking may offer discounts.
- **Taxi:**
    - **Price:** Around 40-50 CHF, depending on traffic and exact destination.
    - **Details:** Taxis are available at the airport, and the journey time is approximately 15-20 minutes, depending on traffic conditions.

Bern Airport (BRN):

- **Bus:**
    - **Price:** Approximately 4 CHF for a one-way ticket.
    - **Details:** Public buses operate from Bern Airport to Bern city center. The journey time is typically around 30 minutes.
- **Taxi:**
    - **Price:** Around 40-50 CHF, depending on traffic and exact destination.
    - **Details:** Taxis are available at the airport, and the journey time is approximately 20-30 minutes, depending on traffic conditions.
- **Shuttle Services:**
    - **Price:** Varies; can range from 20 CHF to 40 CHF or more.
    - **Details:** Shared or private shuttle services may be available, and prices depend on the service provider. Advance booking may offer discounts.
- **Car Rental:**

- **Price:** Varies based on the rental company and type of vehicle.
- **Details:** Car rental services are available at Bern Airport. Prices depend on the rental duration, type of car, and additional services.

Getting Around Switzerland

Transportation in Switzerland is known for its efficiency, reliability, and picturesque journeys through the Alps. There are a myriad ways you can enjoy it cheaply!

Swiss Travel Pass:

Covered in depth above. his pass offers unlimited travel on trains, buses, and boats and provides free admission to many museums.

FlixBus and Similar Services:

Long-distance buses, such as FlixBus, can be more affordable than trains. Prices for FlixBus journeys within Switzerland may start from 15 CHF. Look for discounts and promotions when booking bus tickets.

Off-Peak Travel:
Travel during off-peak hours to benefit from lower fares. Avoiding rush hours can help you save money on both trains and buses. Off-peak train tickets may be around 30-40% cheaper than peak-time fares.

Carsharing:
Explore carsharing options if you plan to travel to less accessible areas. Companies like Mobility or Sharoo offer convenient solutions. Prices vary, but carsharing rates may start from 0.50 CHF per minute or 2 CHF per hour.

Bike Rentals:
n cities and scenic areas, consider renting a bike for a free and eco-friendly mode of transportation. Prices for bike rentals are free in many cities. In small villages prices range from 10 CHF to 30 CHF per day.

Use Gas Price Apps:
Apps like GasBuddy or Fuelio can help you locate gas stations and compare prices before purchasing. Gas in rural parts of Switzerland will be much higher than the cities.

Luxury on a Budget Guide to the Switzerlands Cities and Towns

Zurich

Zurich, Switzerland's largest city, stands proudly on the shores of Lake Zurich, serving as the nation's economic and cultural heartbeat. Recognized for its scenic beauty, robust economy, and cultural vibrancy, Zurich has a compelling story to tell.

In the annals of Zurich's past, traces of Roman influence linger, with Lindenhof, the Roman customs post, marking the city's ancient origins. Zurich joined the Swiss Confederacy in 1351, a move that propelled it into medieval prominence. The 16th century witnessed the city at the forefront of the Protestant Reformation under Ulrich Zwingli. Industrialization in the 19th century ushered in a new era, transforming Zurich into a bustling industrial and financial center.

1. Affordable Accommodation:

Budget Boutique Hotels: Consider staying at boutique hotels that offer luxurious amenities at a fraction of the cost. Options like 25hours Hotel Langstrasse or Hotel Adler offer luxury rooms from 90 CHF.

Hostels with Style: Zurich has hostels that provide a comfortable stay without breaking the bank. Check out places like Hostel Langstars for a budget-friendly yet chic experience.

2. Cheap Eats and drinks:

Street Food and Markets: Explore food markets like Helvetiaplatz Market or Im Viadukt Market for delicious and affordable local eats. Try Swiss specialties such as raclette or fondue from street vendors.

Budget-Friendly Cafes: Visit cozy cafes like Café Henrici or Milchbar for reasonably priced meals and a relaxing atmosphere.

Finding cheap eats in Zurich can be a bit challenging due to its reputation for higher prices, but there are still affordable options available. Keep in mind that prices may vary, and it's a good idea to check the latest information before visiting. Here are a few recommendations:

Rheinfelder Bierhalle
Address: Niederdorfstrasse 76, 8001 Zurich

What to Eat: Traditional Swiss dishes, such as Zürcher Geschnetzeltes (sliced veal in mushroom cream sauce), and hearty pub food.

Opening Times: Daily from 9:00 AM to midnight (kitchen closes at 10:00 PM).

Haus Hiltl - Vegi Restaurant
Address: Sihlstrasse 28, 8001 Zurich

What to Eat: Hiltl claims to be the world's oldest vegetarian restaurant. Enjoy their diverse vegetarian and vegan buffet.

Opening Times: Daily from 6:00 AM to midnight.

Tibits
Address: Seefeldstrasse 2, 8008 Zurich

What to Eat: Vegetarian and vegan buffet with a pay-per-weight system. Mix and match your favorite dishes.

Opening Times: Daily from 7:30 AM to 12:00 AM.

Gelati Tellhof
Address: Tellstrasse 12, 8004 Zurich

What to Eat: Delicious and reasonably priced gelato. Perfect for a sweet treat.

Opening Times: Monday to Saturday from 12:00 PM to 10:00 PM; Sunday from 11:00 AM to 10:00 PM.

Ziegel oh Lac
Address: Stadthausquai 11, 8001 Zurich

What to Eat: Affordable and tasty Middle Eastern cuisine, including falafel and kebabs.

Opening Times: Monday to Saturday from 11:00 AM to 11:00 PM; Sunday from 12:00 PM to 10:00 PM.

Sprüngli Confiserie
Address: Bahnhofstrasse 21, 8001 Zurich

What to Eat: While not the cheapest, Sprüngli is an iconic Swiss patisserie where you can enjoy Luxemburgerli (macarons) or a slice of cake at a relatively reasonable price.

Opening Times: Monday to Friday from 7:00 AM to 6:30 PM; Saturday from 7:00 AM to 5:00 PM.

Cheap Rooftop Bars:

Felsenegg Restaurant & Bar
Address: Felsenegg, 8832 Wollerau (reachable by boat from Zurich)

Tip: Take a boat ride to Felsenegg and enjoy stunning views of Lake Zurich and the Alps. The restaurant and bar offer a unique atmosphere.

Clouds Bistro & Bar
Address: Maagplatz 5, 8005 Zurich

Tip: Head to the 35th floor for the Clouds Bistro & Bar. While it's not the cheapest, it offers a more budget-friendly experience compared to fine dining.

Hiltl Dachterrasse
Address: Bahnhofstrasse 88, 8001 Zurich

Tip: Hiltl Dachterrasse is the rooftop terrace of Haus Hiltl. Enjoy a vegetarian or vegan meal with a view of the city.

Places with Free Live Music:

El Lokal
Address: Gessnerallee 11, 8001 Zurich
Tip: El Lokal is known for its diverse cultural events, including free live music performances. Check their schedule for upcoming gigs.

Kaufleuten
Address: Pelikanplatz, 8001 Zurich
Tip: Kaufleuten is a renowned venue with various events. While some shows may have an entrance fee, they often host free concerts and performances. Check their calendar for details.

Moods im Schiffbau
Address: Pfingstweidstrasse 101, 8005 Zurich
Tip: Moods is a jazz club with a great atmosphere. While some performances may require tickets, they occasionally host free jam sessions and smaller gigs.

Barfussbar
Address: Stadthausquai 11, 8001 Zurich
Tip: Barfussbar is a popular summer spot along the Limmat River. Enjoy the relaxed atmosphere with occasional free live music.

Bogen F
Address: Viaduktstrasse, 8005 Zurich
Tip: Bogen F is part of the Viadukt complex, known for its vibrant atmosphere. They host various events, including free concerts. Check their schedule for details.

3. Luxury Experiences for Less

Lake Zurich Cruise: Embark on a luxurious cruise along Lake Zurich, taking in the picturesque views of the city and the Alps. Prices start at around 25 CHF for a scenic boat ride.

Lindt Chocolate Experience: Immerse yourself in the world of Swiss chocolate at the Lindt Chocolate Factory in Kilchberg. Enjoy a guided tour for approximately 10 CHF and savor exquisite chocolate creations.

Old Town Walking Tour: Uncover Zurich's medieval charm on a guided walking tour through the Old Town. Many tours are available for around 20-30 CHF, providing insights into the city's fascinating history.

Uetliberg Panorama Train: Ascend Uetliberg Mountain in style by taking the panorama train for approximately 15 CHF. Revel in breathtaking views of Zurich and the surrounding landscapes.

Swiss National Museum: Immerse yourself in Swiss history at the Swiss National Museum. Admission is around 10 CHF, granting you access to a treasure trove of artifacts and exhibits.

Kunsthaus Zurich: Experience the city's art scene at Kunsthaus Zurich, where admission is approximately 20 CHF. Marvel at works by Swiss and international artists spanning centuries.

Grossmünster Towers: Climb the iconic Grossmünster Towers for panoramic views of Zurich. Tickets are roughly 5 CHF, providing a budget-friendly way to admire the city skyline.

Botanical Garden Entrance: Explore the Zurich University Botanical Garden for a modest fee of around 6 CHF. Discover diverse plant collections and serene green spaces.

Felsenegg Cable Car: Glide over Lake Zurich on the Felsenegg Cable Car, offering spectacular vistas. The round-trip fare is approximately 30 CHF, including breathtaking views of the city.

Boat Rental on Lake Zurich: Enjoy a leisurely boat ride on Lake Zurich by renting a rowboat for about 20 CHF per hour. Bask in the tranquility of the lake at your own pace.

Rietberg Museum: Dive into world cultures at the Rietberg Museum for around 15 CHF. Marvel at art and artifacts from Asia, Africa, and the Americas in a serene park setting.

Zurich Zoo: Spend a day at Zurich Zoo for roughly 30 CHF, exploring themed habitats and engaging with wildlife. It's a budget-friendly way to enjoy a day of family-friendly luxury.

Augusto Giacometti Frescoes: Admire the stunning frescoes by Augusto Giacometti at the Kunsthaus Zurich. Entrance is approximately 20 CHF, offering a glimpse into Swiss artistic mastery.

Swiss Alpine Museum: Immerse yourself in the alpine heritage at the Swiss Alpine Museum for around 12 CHF. Discover the cultural richness of Switzerland's mountainous regions.

Lake Zurich Dinner Cruise: Elevate your dining experience with a dinner cruise on Lake Zurich, with prices starting at around 90 CHF. Indulge in gourmet cuisine while surrounded by the city lights.

Opera House Backstage Tour: Unveil the magic behind the scenes with a backstage tour of the Zurich Opera House for about 15 CHF. Gain insights into the world of opera and theater.

Zurich Film Festival Screening: Attend a film screening at the Zurich Film Festival for approximately 20 CHF. Immerse yourself in the world of cinema during this annual cultural celebration.

Fine Dining at Lindenhofkeller: Delight in a gourmet experience at Lindenhofkeller, one of Zurich's oldest restaurants. Enjoy a sumptuous meal with prices starting around 30 CHF.

Opera or Ballet Performance: Attend a world-class opera or ballet performance at the Opernhaus Zurich. Ticket prices vary, but affordable options are often available for as low as 40 CHF.

Swiss Fondue Experience: Indulge in a quintessential Swiss fondue experience at Swiss Chuchi. Prices start at around 25 CHF, allowing you to savor this iconic dish in a cozy atmosphere.

4. Free Things to Do:

Lake Zurich Promenade: Take a leisurely stroll along Lake Zurich's promenade, enjoying beautiful views of the city and the Alps. It's a perfect free activity for a relaxing afternoon. The lake witnessed the establishment of the Celtic-Roman town of "Lindenhof," and today, you can spot the Quaibrücke, a bridge with historical significance, as you enjoy the panoramic views.

Old Town Exploration: Wander through Zurich's charming Old Town (Altstadt) to discover historic sites, cobblestone streets, and vibrant street art, all for free. The Grossmünster towers stand as a testament to the Reformation led by Zwingli. Don't miss the Niederdorf area, once the bohemian quarter, and the St. Peter's Church clock face, Europe's largest.

Free Museum Entry: Many museums offer free entry on the first Wednesday of each month. Take advantage of this to explore cultural institutions like the Swiss National Museum without spending a dime.

Lindenhof: Once a Roman castle, Lindenhof offers more than just views. Discover the Lindenhof's "Peace Tree," symbolizing the end of a medieval feud, and the chess tables, a tradition dating back to the 19th century.

Free Walking Tours: Join a walking tour to uncover Zurich's secrets, including the Cabaret Voltaire, the birthplace of the Dada movement that revolutionized modern art, and the Rathaus, the medieval town hall.

Grossmünster: Admire the Grossmünster's Romanesque architecture and climb its towers. Legend has it that Charlemagne discovered the graves of Zurich's patron saints, Felix and Regula, here, marking the birth of the city.

Kunsthalle Zurich: Step into Kunsthalle Zurich to see contemporary art. The building itself, a former brewery, preserves industrial history, while exhibitions often showcase the city's influence on Dadaism and modern art movements.

Botanical Garden: Founded in 1837, the Botanical Garden reveals Zurich's dedication to scientific research. Look for the "Evolution Garden," showcasing plant evolution, and the historical greenhouse from the late 19th century.

Window Shopping on Bahnhofstrasse: While strolling Bahnhofstrasse, notice the Fraumünster Church's stained glass windows by artist Marc Chagall, a striking blend of modern art in a medieval setting, reflecting Zurich's artistic diversity.

Uetliberg Mountain: Hike up Uetliberg, a vantage point since the Roman era. Explore the Uetliberg TV tower, a relic of early broadcasting history, and the Uetliberg observatory, which contributed to the understanding of the Alps.

ETH Zurich Campus: Visit the ETH Zurich campus, where Einstein once studied. The Polyterrasse offers a stunning panorama of Zurich and the Alps, and the Arch-Tech building showcases Zurich's architectural innovation.

Limmat River: Along the Limmat, discover medieval water wells and the Rathaus bridge. Dive into the history of Swiss guilds and trade that shaped Zurich as a vibrant economic center.

Zurich University Botanical Garden: Established in 1974, the Botanical Garden features themed gardens, like the Alpine Garden and the Scented Garden. Look out for the historical "Villa Boveri" building, a remnant of Zurich's industrial past.

Free Events at Bellevue Square: Bellevue Square, a historical gathering place, hosts events. Keep an eye out for the Sechseläuten festival, symbolizing the end of winter, and the Christmas market, a festive tradition.

Rietberg Museum Park: Adjacent to the Rietberg Museum, the park houses sculptures and a Chinese Garden. Spot the "Fountain of the Muses," a 19th-century masterpiece, and the "Dreaming Spires" sculpture by Igor Mitoraj.

Chinese Garden Zurich: Explore the Chinese Garden, a gift from Zurich's sister city Kunming. Admire the Nine Dragon Wall, symbolizing protection, and the Chinese Pavilion, blending traditional architecture with Zurich's greenery.

Street Food Market at Helvetiaplatz: Helvetiaplatz, historically a melting pot, hosts a diverse street food market. Taste global flavors while soaking in Zurich's multicultural history, from its industrial past to the present.

5. Cultural Events:

Public Art Installations: Zurich often hosts free public art installations and performances. Check the city's event calendar for information on cultural events that won't cost you a cent.
Free Concerts and Festivals: Keep an eye out for free concerts and festivals happening in parks or public spaces. Zurich frequently hosts open-air events during the warmer months.

Lectures and Talks: Some cultural institutions and universities in Zurich host free lectures, talks, and panel discussions on various topics. Check the schedules of institutions like the University of Zurich or ETH Zurich for public events.

5. Budget-Friendly Transport:

City Bikes: Opt for Zurich's bike-sharing program to explore the city for free. It's a sustainable and cost-effective way to travel between attractions.

Public Transportation Pass: Invest in a Zurich Card, offering unlimited 2nd class travel by tram, bus, train, boat, cableway, and funicular within the city. It also provides free or discounted entry to many museums.

RECAP

Zurich Costs	Money saving tips
Accommodation	Boutique hotels (e.g., 25hours Hotel Langstrasse, Hotel Adler), hostels (e.g., Zurich Youth Hostel), budget-friendly options on booking platforms.
Transportation	Utilize public transportation such as trams and buses (ZürichCARD for unlimited rides), explore on foot for city center attractions.
Dining	Enjoy local markets like Viadukt Market, cafes such as Milchbar, affordable eateries like Hiltl for vegetarian options.
Sightseeing	Purchase ZurichCARD for discounts on museums and attractions, explore Old Town (Altstadt) and Lake Zurich on your own.
Entertainment	Attend free or low-cost events, relax in public spaces like Lindenhof or Uetliberg for panoramic views.
Shopping	Visit local markets like Flohmarkt Kanzlei or outlets like Outlet City Metzingen for budget-friendly shopping.
Day Trips	Plan self-guided day trips to Rhine Falls, Lucerne, or Rapperswil, using cost-effective transportation options.
Currency Exchange	Withdraw local currency from ATMs for better rates, avoid high fees by using local banks.
Timing	Visit during shoulder seasons (spring or fall) for a balance of good weather and lower prices.
Technology	Use budget-friendly apps like SBB Mobile for public transportation, Maps.me for offline navigation, and local deal apps.

Geneva

Nestled along the shores of Lake Geneva, the city of Geneva stands as a beacon of diplomacy, culture, and international cooperation. Geneva has a rich history dating back to Roman times, but its modern identity is largely shaped by its role in international diplomacy. The city's strategic location at the confluence of the Rhône River and Lake Geneva made it a hub for trade and commerce. In the 16th century, Geneva became a center of the Protestant Reformation under the leadership of John Calvin. The city played a key role in the development of international humanitarian law, hosting the International Committee of the Red Cross (ICRC) since its founding in 1863. Geneva has also been a focal point for diplomatic activities and is home to numerous international organizations, including the United Nations and the World Health Organization. Today, it continues to be a global city known for its cultural diversity, financial institutions, and commitment to human rights.

1. Affordable Accommodation:

Budget-Friendly Hotels: Geneva has several budget-friendly hotels offering comfortable stays. Consider Hotel Edelweiss or Hotel ibis Genève Centre Nations for a balance of quality and affordability.
Hostels with Charm: Explore stylish hostels like City Hostel Geneva for a cost-effective and pleasant accommodation experience.

2. Cheap Eats:

Ethnic Cuisine in Paquis: Visit the Paquis district for affordable and diverse ethnic cuisine. You'll find budget-friendly options from Middle Eastern to Asian flavors.
Local Markets: Head to Plainpalais Market or Les Halles de l'Île for fresh and reasonably priced local produce, snacks, and meals.

Luxury for Less

Jet d'Eau Boat Tour: Cruise the waters of Lake Geneva for around 20 CHF, offering a unique perspective of the iconic Jet d'Eau fountain.
St. Pierre Cathedral Towers: Ascend the towers of St. Pierre Cathedral for panoramic views of Geneva at approximately 5 CHF. Uncover the history of this landmark, dating back to the Roman era.
Paddleboarding on Lake Geneva: Experience the serenity of Lake Geneva by renting a paddleboard for around 20 CHF per hour. Glide across the crystal-clear waters with the cityscape as your backdrop.
Parc La Perle du Lac Boat Rental: Rent a rowboat at Parc La Perle du Lac for a tranquil experience at about 10 CHF per hour. Enjoy the scenic beauty of this lakeside park.
United Nations Office at Geneva Tour: Explore the United Nations headquarters with a guided tour for around 12 CHF. Gain insights into global diplomacy and visit key chambers.

Maison Tavel: Visit Maison Tavel, Switzerland's oldest house, for free. Delve into Geneva's medieval past in this historic setting.

Bain des Pâquis Wellness: Relax at Bain des Pâquis, a lakeside public bath, for approximately 2 CHF. Enjoy the saunas, Turkish baths, and the unique atmosphere.

International Red Cross and Red Crescent Museum: Discover humanitarian history at the International Red Cross and Red Crescent Museum for around 15 CHF. Engage with immersive exhibits on humanitarian efforts.

Reformation Wall: Admire the Reformation Wall in Parc des Bastions for free. This monumental sculpture commemorates the leaders of the Protestant Reformation.

Botanical Gardens Entry: Explore the Geneva Botanical Gardens for about 6 CHF. Wander through themed gardens and enjoy the tranquility of this green oasis.

Quartier des Grottes Street Art Tour: Take a self-guided walking tour through Quartier des Grottes to appreciate vibrant street art. This budget-friendly exploration offers a unique perspective on the city.

Musée d'Art et d'Histoire: Dive into art and history at the Musée d'Art et d'Histoire for around 10 CHF. Marvel at its diverse collection of paintings, sculptures, and decorative arts.

Patek Philippe Museum: While the museum has an entrance fee, visit Plainpalais Flea Market nearby for free. Browse through eclectic items and soak in the market's vibrant atmosphere.

Rue du Rhône Window Shopping: Stroll along Rue du Rhône and admire the luxury boutiques. While shopping may be a splurge, window shopping is a delightful and free activity.

Parc Bertrand Bandstand Concerts: Enjoy free concerts at the Parc Bertrand bandstand during the summer months. Immerse yourself in live music amidst a scenic park setting.

Jardin Anglais Floral Clock: Admire the L'Horloge Fleurie (Floral Clock) at Jardin Anglais for free. This meticulously crafted clock is a floral masterpiece.

Ariana Museum Gardens: While the museum may have an entrance fee, explore the gardens of the Ariana Museum for free. Marvel at sculptures and enjoy a peaceful ambiance.

Bastions Park Chessboards: Engage in a game of chess at the giant outdoor chessboards in Bastions Park. This recreational activity is free and located in a charming park setting.

Boat Cruise to Yvoire: Take a budget-friendly boat cruise to Yvoire, a medieval French village on the shores of Lake Geneva, for around 30 CHF. Enjoy a day trip to this charming destination.

Visit Carouge: Explore the bohemian district of Carouge, known for its artisan boutiques and Mediterranean flair. Stroll through its charming streets, and window shop for unique finds.

3. Free Things to Do:

Jet d'Eau and Lake Geneva: Enjoy the iconic Jet d'Eau fountain and stroll along Lake Geneva's shores for breathtaking views of the city and the Alps.

Parks and Gardens: Explore Parc La Bâtie or Parc des Bastions for tranquil green spaces perfect for a budget-friendly day out.

Free Museum Days: Take advantage of free entry days at museums like the Natural History Museum and the Museum of Art and History.

4. Cultural Events:

Public Art Installations: Geneva often features free public art installations. Keep an eye out for temporary exhibits and sculptures throughout the city.
Music Festivals: Check the local event calendar for free music festivals and concerts in parks or public spaces, especially during the summer months.

5. Budget-Friendly Transport:

Geneva Transport Card: Many hotels offer a free Geneva Transport Card, providing complimentary use of public transportation, including buses and boats. Take advantage of this for an affordable way to explore the city.
Walking Tours: Geneva is a walkable city, and you can explore its charm on foot. Consider self-guided walking tours to discover the city's landmarks without spending on transportation.
By incorporating these tips, you can experience the elegance of Geneva without exceeding your budget, enjoying its scenic beauty, cultural attractions, and diverse culinary offerings.

Aspect	Money saving tips
Accommodation	Budget-friendly hotels like Ibis Styles Geneve Gare, hostels such as City Hostel Geneva, or consider Airbnb for affordable options.
Transportation	Utilize public transportation with Geneva Transport Card for trams and buses, explore the city on foot, or rent a bike for a cost-effective option.
Dining	Enjoy budget-friendly options at Plainpalais Market, cafes like La Clémence, and affordable eateries like Chez Ma Cousine for rotisserie chicken.
Sightseeing	Take advantage of the Geneva Pass for discounted entry to museums and attractions, explore the Old Town (Vieille Ville) and Jet d'Eau independently.
Entertainment	Attend free concerts at Parc La Bâtie, relax by Lake Geneva, or explore the International Red Cross and Red Crescent Museum.
Shopping	Visit Plainpalais Flea Market for unique finds, and explore Rue du Mont-Blanc for budget-friendly shopping.
Day Trips	Plan a budget-friendly day trip to Mont Salève or Yvoire by using public transportation options.
Currency Exchange	Withdraw local currency from ATMs for better rates, avoid high fees by using local banks.
Timing	Visit during the shoulder seasons (spring or fall) for pleasant weather and potentially lower prices.
Technology	Use budget-friendly apps like TPG (Transport Public Genevois) for public transportation, Maps.me for navigation, and local deal apps.

Lucerne

Lucerne is a charming city that captivates visitors with its medieval architecture, stunning lakeside setting, and a sense of timeless beauty. Founded in the 8th century, Lucerne's strategic location on Lake Lucerne and its proximity to the Swiss Alps contributed to its early economic importance. The city's iconic Kapellbrücke (Chapel Bridge) and Water Tower, constructed in the 14th century, stand as enduring symbols of Lucerne's medieval charm. During the Reformation, Lucerne remained a stronghold of Catholicism. In the 19th century, the arrival of the railroad solidified its position as a vital transportation hub. Lucerne's stunning landscapes, including the nearby Rigi and Pilatus mountains, have long made it a favorite destination for tourists. Today, Lucerne seamlessly blends its historical charm with a vibrant cultural scene and is celebrated for its role as a gateway to Switzerland's scenic wonders.

1. Affordable Accommodation:

Budget-Friendly Hotels: Explore options like Hotel des Balances or Hotel Falken for affordable yet charming accommodations in the heart of Lucerne's Old Town.
Guesthouses and Inns: Consider staying in guesthouses or inns like Hotel Alpha or Hotel Rothaus for a cozy and budget-friendly experience.

2. Cheap Eats:

Street Food at Weinmarkt: Weinmarkt square in Lucerne offers a variety of street food options. Grab a quick and affordable bite while exploring the historic Old Town.
Local Bakeries: Visit local bakeries for fresh pastries and sandwiches. Bakeries like Bachmann are known for quality at reasonable prices.

Luxury for less

Chapel Bridge (Kapellbrücke) Walk: Stroll along the iconic Chapel Bridge, one of Lucerne's landmarks, offering stunning views of the Old Town and surrounding mountains. This is a delightful free activity.

Lake Lucerne Cruise: Embark on a boat cruise on Lake Lucerne, enjoying the scenic beauty of the surrounding mountains. Prices start at around 30 CHF for a round-trip cruise.

Lucerne City Walking Tour: Join a guided walking tour of Lucerne's Old Town to uncover its medieval charm and learn about historical landmarks. Many tours are available for around 20-30 CHF.

Lion Monument: Admire the poignant Lion Monument (Löwendenkmal), a sculpted memorial, which can be explored for free. Learn about the history behind this iconic symbol.

Swiss Museum of Transport (Verkehrshaus der Schweiz): Explore the Swiss Museum of Transport for approximately 32 CHF. Delve into Switzerland's transportation history through interactive exhibits.

Rigi Mountain Day Trip: Take a budget-friendly day trip to Mount Rigi, often referred to as the "Queen of the Mountains." Train and boat packages are available for around 60 CHF.

Old Town Shopping: Wander through Lucerne's Old Town and explore its charming streets filled with boutique shops. While shopping may incur costs, window shopping is a delightful free activity.

Glacier Garden (Gletschergarten): Visit the Glacier Garden for approximately 15 CHF. Discover ancient rock formations and the Mirror Maze in this unique garden setting.

Lucerne Art Museum (Kunstmuseum Luzern): Explore the Lucerne Art Museum for around 20 CHF. Immerse yourself in a collection spanning Swiss and international contemporary art.

Picnic at Lake Lucerne: Enjoy a budget-friendly picnic at Lake Lucerne's shores. Purchase local produce from markets and savor a scenic meal with mountain views.

Water Tower (Wasserturm) Climb: Ascend the Water Tower on the Chapel Bridge for about 8 CHF. Gain panoramic views of Lucerne and the surrounding landscapes.

Glacier Paradise (Eisgrotte): Experience the Glacier Paradise, a natural ice cave, as part of a trip to Mount Titlis. Prices for the excursion start at around 80 CHF.

Richard Wagner Museum: While the museum may have an entrance fee, enjoy the free lakeside ambiance near the Richard Wagner Museum in Tribschen.

Lucerne Lake Promenade: Take a leisurely walk along the Lucerne Lake Promenade, offering breathtaking views of the surrounding mountains and lake. This is a free and rejuvenating activity.

Lucerne Theatre (Luzerner Theater): Attend a budget-friendly performance at the Lucerne Theatre. Ticket prices vary, but affordable options are often available for as low as 20 CHF.

Pilatus Mountain Cable Car: Take the cable car to Mount Pilatus for around 38 CHF. Revel in panoramic views and explore the mountain's attractions.

Hofkirche (Church of St. Leodegar): Visit the Hofkirche, also known as the Church of St. Leodegar, for free. Explore the historic church and its surroundings.

Swiss Chocolate Adventure: Indulge in a Swiss Chocolate Adventure at the Swiss Museum of Transport for around 32 CHF. Immerse yourself in the world of Swiss chocolate.

Lucerne Hiking Trails: Discover budget-friendly hiking trails around Lucerne, such as the Hammetschwand Trail. Experience the region's natural beauty without breaking the bank.

Alpineum: Explore the Alpineum, an exhibition dedicated to Switzerland's Alpine region, for about 15 CHF. Learn about the culture, flora, and fauna of the Swiss Alps.

4. Cultural Events:

Open-Air Concerts: Lucerne often hosts free open-air concerts during the summer months. Check local event listings for opportunities to enjoy music against the backdrop of the city's scenic beauty.

Art Exhibitions: Explore free art exhibitions at venues like the Kunstmuseum Luzern or the Richard Wagner Museum.

5. Budget-Friendly Transport:

Lucerne Visitor Card: Many hotels provide guests with a Lucerne Visitor Card, offering free use of buses and discounts on boats and cable cars. Use this card for affordable and convenient transportation.

Walk around Lake Lucerne: Take a leisurely stroll around Lake Lucerne. It's a cost-free way to appreciate the breathtaking views of the lake and surrounding mountains.

By combining these recommendations, you can savor the enchanting atmosphere of Lucerne on a budget, enjoying its historic charm, natural beauty, and cultural offerings without compromising on luxury.

Aspect	Money saving tips
Accommodation	Consider budget-friendly hotels like Hotel Alpha, hostels such as Jailhotel Loewengraben, or explore affordable options on booking platforms.
Transportation	Use the Tell-Pass for discounted public transportation, take advantage of free walking tours in the city, and explore the Old Town on foot.
Dining	Enjoy budget-friendly options at St. Leodegar, cafes like Bucherer, and affordable eateries like Rathaus Brauerei for Swiss specialties.
Sightseeing	Use the Tell-Pass for discounts on boat rides, cable cars, and museums. Explore Chapel Bridge (Kapellbrücke) and Water Tower (Wasserturm) independently.
Entertainment	Attend free events at the KKL Luzern (Culture and Convention Centre Lucerne) or enjoy the scenery at Lake Lucerne.
Shopping	Explore budget-friendly shopping at Hertensteinstrasse and Nadelberg for souvenirs and local finds.
Day Trips	Plan a cost-effective day trip to Mount Pilatus or Mount Rigi using the Tell-Pass and public transportation options.
Currency Exchange	Withdraw local currency from ATMs for better rates, avoid high fees by using local banks.
Timing	Visit during the shoulder seasons (spring or fall) for pleasant weather and potentially lower prices.
Technology	Use budget-friendly apps like SBB Mobile for transportation, Maps.me for navigation, and local deal apps for discounts.

Bern

Bern, the capital city of Switzerland, is a UNESCO World Heritage site known for its well-preserved medieval old town, charming architecture, and rich history. It has a storied history that dates back to its founding in the 12th century. Established around 1191 by Duke Berthold V of Zähringen, the city is situated along the Aare River. Bern's medieval Old Town, a UNESCO World Heritage Site, features well-preserved architecture, including the iconic Zytglogge clock tower and the Federal Palace. In the 16th century, the city became a center of the Protestant Reformation under the leadership of reformer Berchtold Haller and others. The bear, a symbol of the city, is associated with the legend of the city's founder. Bern played a crucial role in the development of the Swiss Confederacy and became the de facto capital in 1848 when the modern Swiss federal state was established. Today, Bern stands as a testament to its medieval heritage, offering a harmonious

1. Affordable Accommodation:

Quaint Guesthouses: Consider staying at guesthouses like Hotel Nydeck or Hotel Glocke for budget-friendly options in Bern's charming Old Town.
Budget-Friendly Hostels: Hostel Bern Backpackers Marzili and Bern Youth Hostel offer affordable accommodations with a youthful atmosphere.

2. Cheap Eats:

Market Snacking: Visit the Zytglogge clock tower area for local markets and affordable snacks. Try Swiss specialties like Rösti or Bernese Oberland cheese.
Student Hangouts: Explore the Länggass district for budget-friendly eateries popular among students. These spots offer a mix of international and local cuisine at reasonable prices.

3. Luxury for less

Zytglogge Clock Tower Visit: Marvel at the Zytglogge Clock Tower in the heart of Bern's Old Town for free. Witness the animated figures and the intricate astronomical clock.
Bern Munster Tower Climb: Ascend the Bern Munster Tower for panoramic views of the city. The entrance fee is approximately 5 CHF, offering a budget-friendly way to enjoy the skyline.
Einstein House Tour: Visit the Einstein House for around 6 CHF. Explore the living quarters where Albert Einstein formulated his famous theory of relativity.
Bear Park Visit: Discover the Bear Park, a sanctuary for bears located near the Old Town, for approximately 15 CHF. Learn about the conservation efforts and observe the bears in a natural environment.
Federal Palace (Bundeshaus) Tour: Join a guided tour of the Federal Palace for about 20 CHF. Explore the Swiss Parliament building and gain insights into Switzerland's political history.

Gurten Funicular Ride: Take a funicular ride to Gurten, Bern's local mountain, for stunning panoramic views. The round-trip ticket is approximately 38 CHF, including access to the viewing platform.
Paul Klee Center: Explore the Paul Klee Center for around 20 CHF. Immerse yourself in the works of the renowned Swiss artist Paul Klee and temporary exhibitions.
Rosengarten (Rose Garden) Visit: Enjoy a leisurely visit to the Rosengarten for free. Admire the blooming roses and panoramic views of Bern's Old Town.
Bern Historical Museum: Discover the Bern Historical Museum for around 15 CHF. Delve into the city's history through a vast collection of artifacts, art, and exhibitions.
Zentrum Paul Klee Park: While the museum has an entrance fee, the surrounding Zentrum Paul Klee Park offers walking trails and green spaces for free. Enjoy a peaceful stroll.
Bern UNESCO World Heritage Site Walking Tour: Join a UNESCO World Heritage Site walking tour for around 20-30 CHF. Explore the well-preserved medieval Old Town and its architectural treasures.
Swiss Alpine Museum Visit: Explore the Swiss Alpine Museum for about 12 CHF. Gain insights into the culture, nature, and history of the Swiss Alps.
Bern Historical Tram Ride: Experience a historical tram ride through Bern for approximately 10 CHF. Travel in style and learn about the city's heritage.
Nydegg Church: Visit Nydegg Church for free. Admire the Gothic architecture and enjoy a peaceful moment in this historic church.
Bern Botanical Garden Entry: Explore the Bern Botanical Garden for around 7 CHF. Wander through diverse plant collections and themed gardens.
Kornhauskeller Dinner: Dine at Kornhauskeller, a historic cellar restaurant in the Old Town. While it may not be budget-friendly, indulging in Swiss cuisine in this iconic setting is a luxurious experience.
Thun Castle Day Trip: Take a day trip to Thun Castle for around 25 CHF. Explore the castle's museum and enjoy views of Lake Thun and the surrounding Alps.
Bern River Aare Walk: Take a scenic walk along the River Aare for free. Enjoy the picturesque landscapes and the city's riverside charm.
Eiger North Face Viewing: Take a day trip to Grindelwald and view the Eiger North Face. Train tickets to Grindelwald start at around 50 CHF.
Schwarzsee (Black Lake) Hike: Explore the Schwarzsee hiking trail for free. Discover the natural beauty of the region and enjoy a peaceful hike.

4. Cultural Events and History:

Zentrum Paul Klee: Visit the free outdoor area of Zentrum Paul Klee, dedicated to the renowned Swiss painter. It's a cultural space with sculptures and beautiful grounds.
Bern Historical Museum: Take advantage of free entry on the first Thursday of each month to explore the Bern Historical Museum, showcasing the city's rich history and culture.

5. Budget-Friendly Transport:

Bern Ticket: Many hotels provide guests with a Bern Ticket, offering free use of public transportation within the city. Use trams and buses to navigate Bern without straining your budget.
Walkable Old Town: Bern's Old Town is compact and easily explored on foot. Wander through the cobbled streets to discover the Zytglogge, the Federal Palace, and the Bear Park.

History of Bern:

Founded in 1191: Bern, the capital of Switzerland, was founded in 1191. The city's name is believed to originate from the German word "Bär," meaning bear, and legend has it that the city was named after the first animal Duke Berchtold V encountered on a hunting expedition – a bear.
UNESCO World Heritage Site: The Old Town of Bern is a UNESCO World Heritage Site, boasting well-preserved medieval architecture, including the iconic Zytglogge clock tower and the Federal Palace.
Epicenter of Swiss Politics: Bern has been the political center of Switzerland since the country's foundation in 1848. The Federal Palace is home to the Swiss Federal Assembly and Federal Council.
By blending these budget-friendly tips with Bern's rich history, you can immerse yourself in the city's cultural tapestry without overspending, making your visit both affordable and enriching.

Aspect	Money saving tips
Accommodation	Consider budget-friendly hotels like Hotel Bristol, hostels such as Bern Backpackers, or explore affordable options on booking platforms.
Transportation	Utilize the Bern Ticket for free public transportation within the city, explore the Old Town on foot, and rent a bike for a cost-effective option.
Dining	Enjoy budget-friendly options at the Federal Square (Bundesplatz) food stalls, cafes like Einstein Kaffee, and affordable eateries like Gelateria di Berna for ice cream.
Sightseeing	Take advantage of the Bern Ticket for free entry to the Bern Historical Museum and other attractions. Explore the Zytglogge clock tower and Bear Park independently.
Entertainment	Attend free events in the Old Town or enjoy the Aare Riverbanks for a relaxing day out.
Shopping	Explore budget-friendly shopping at the Kramgasse and Nydeggasse for unique finds and souvenirs.
Day Trips	Plan a cost-effective day trip to the Emmental region or Thun using the efficient Swiss public transportation system.
Currency Exchange	Withdraw local currency from ATMs for better rates, avoid high fees by using local banks.
Timing	Visit during the shoulder seasons (spring or fall) for pleasant weather and potentially lower prices.
Technology	Use budget-friendly apps like Bernmobil for public transportation, Maps.me for navigation, and local deal apps for discounts.

St. Gallen

Collegiate Church

This vibrant city, founded in the 7th century, seamlessly blends medieval charm with modern sophistication. Renowned for its UNESCO World Heritage-listed Abbey Library, St. Gallen is a haven for history enthusiasts and literary connoisseurs alike. The city's Old Town, with its labyrinthine cobblestone streets and well-preserved architecture, invites visitors to stroll through centuries of stories. St. Gallen is not merely a repository of the past; it's a dynamic hub of academia, boasting the prestigious University of St. Gallen. Surrounded by rolling hills and complemented by a network of crystal-clear lakes, the city offers a harmonious balance between urban vitality and natural serenity.

Affordable Accommodation:

Opt for boutique hotels or charming bed and breakfasts in the city center. Look for deals on booking websites or consider staying slightly outside the main tourist areas for lower rates.

Culinary Delights without the Price Tag:
Explore local markets like the St. Gallen Neudorf Market for fresh produce and regional specialties. Create your own picnic with Swiss cheese, bread, and fresh fruits.

Luxury for less

Abbey Library of St. Gallen:
Immerse yourself in the opulence of the Abbey Library, a UNESCO World Heritage Site. While there may be a small fee to enter, the experience of exploring this historic library is well worth it.

Old Town Stroll:
Wander through the charming Old Town with its medieval architecture and cobblestone streets. The ambiance is rich with history and provides a luxurious feel at no cost.

Three Ponds (Drei Weieren):
Enjoy the tranquility of the Three Ponds, a scenic spot within walking distance of the city center. The breathtaking views are a luxurious experience without spending a penny.

St. Gallen Cathedral:
Visit the St. Gallen Cathedral, an architectural masterpiece. While entrance to the church is free, the interior's grandeur will make you feel like you're in a luxury setting.

St. Gallen Art Museum:
Take advantage of free admission days or discounted rates at the St. Gallen Art Museum. Explore contemporary and classical art in an elegant setting.

Müller'sches Volksbad:
Relax in the Müller'sches Volksbad, a public bath with a historic ambiance. The affordable entrance fee grants you access to a unique and luxurious bathing experience.

City Parks and Gardens:
Spend an afternoon in the various parks and gardens scattered throughout St. Gallen. The green spaces provide a serene and luxurious escape from the urban hustle.

Klosterhof:
Experience the Klosterhof, a courtyard near the Abbey with a tranquil atmosphere. Enjoy the surroundings and take a moment to unwind in this picturesque spot.

Lokremise:
Visit Lokremise, a cultural center housed in a former locomotive depot. Check for free events, exhibitions, or performances that provide a taste of luxury without the high price tag.

Outdoor Yoga or Meditation:
Practice yoga or meditation in one of St. Gallen's parks or open spaces. Find a moment of serenity and luxury in the midst of nature.

Lake Constance Promenade:
Take a short trip to the Lake Constance promenade. The stunning views and fresh air offer a luxurious experience without spending much.

St. Gallen Markets:
Explore local markets like the St. Gallen Neudorf Market. While you may be tempted to purchase local delicacies, simply strolling through the market feels like a high-end shopping experience.

Free City Tours:
Look for free city tours organized by local guides. It's a fantastic way to learn about the city's history and architecture without breaking the bank.

Rhine Falls Day Trip:
Plan a day trip to Rhine Falls, Europe's largest waterfall. While transportation may have a cost, witnessing the awe-inspiring natural wonder is a luxurious experience in itself.

St. Laurenzen Church:
Visit St. Laurenzen Church, an architectural gem. Enjoy the tranquility and beauty of the church's interior without spending a dime.

Botanical Garden:
Explore the Botanical Garden at the University of St. Gallen. The diverse plant collections and well-maintained grounds provide a peaceful and luxurious escape.

University of St. Gallen Campus:
Take a leisurely stroll through the University of St. Gallen campus. The modern architecture and well-groomed surroundings create an atmosphere of sophistication.

Gallusplatz Square:
Spend time at Gallusplatz Square, a lively gathering place. Enjoy the vibrant atmosphere and perhaps indulge in a coffee from a local café while people-watching.

City Views from St. Georgen Hill:
Hike up St. Georgen Hill for panoramic views of the city. The feeling of accomplishment and the breathtaking scenery provide a luxurious experience without any cost.

Public Concerts or Performances:
Check for public concerts or performances happening in the city. St. Gallen often hosts events that allow you to enjoy cultural experiences for free or at a minimal cost.

Free and Low-Cost Attractions:
Visit the Abbey of St. Gallen, a UNESCO World Heritage Site, and explore its beautiful library. Entrance to the church is free, and the library has a nominal fee.

Take a stroll through the charming Old Town with its cobblestone streets and medieval architecture. Enjoy the historical ambiance without spending a dime.

Cultural Experiences:
Check out the St. Gallen Art Museum, which often has free admission days or discounted rates during specific hours.

Attend local events and festivals, many of which are free and offer a taste of the city's culture. Keep an eye on community boards and online event calendars for updates.

Scenic Nature Escapes:
Hike the nearby hills and enjoy panoramic views of St. Gallen. The Drei Weieren (Three Ponds) is a scenic spot within walking distance of the city center.

Take a boat ride on Lake Constance, just a short drive from St. Gallen. Enjoy the stunning landscapes without spending a fortune.

Public Transportation:

Use the efficient and well-connected public transportation system to explore the city and surrounding areas. Consider purchasing a transportation pass for additional savings.

Walking is also a great way to discover St. Gallen's hidden gems. The compact size of the city makes it easy to explore on foot.

Spa and Wellness on a Budget:

Look for day spa packages or wellness centers that offer discounted rates during off-peak hours.

Consider exploring the public thermal baths in the region for a relaxing and budget-friendly spa experience.

Conclusion:

Interlaken

Interlaken, nestled between Lake Thun and Lake Brienz, is a picturesque town in the Bernese Oberland region of Switzerland. Its history is closely tied to its stunning natural surroundings and the development of tourism in the Swiss Alps. The name "Interlaken" translates to "between the lakes," emphasizing its idyllic location. In the 19th century, Interlaken gained popularity as a tourist destination, attracting visitors seeking the breathtaking views of the Jungfrau, Eiger, and Mönch mountains. The advent of the railway in the late 19th century further facilitated tourism growth. Interlaken has since evolved into a hub for outdoor enthusiasts, offering activities such as hiking, skiing, and paragliding. Its charming streets, historic hotels, and proximity to iconic Swiss landscapes make Interlaken a quintessential destination that seamlessly combines history with the allure of the Alps.

1. Affordable Accommodation:

Budget-Friendly Hostels: Interlaken offers hostels like Backpackers Villa Sonnenhof and Balmers Hostel, providing affordable stays with a lively atmosphere.
Guesthouses in Unterseen: Consider staying in the neighboring town of Unterseen, where guesthouses like Hotel Beausite offer a quieter and budget-friendly alternative.

2. Cheap Eats:

Street Food at Hoheweg: Explore Hoheweg, the main street in Interlaken, for affordable street food and snacks. Grab a quick bite while enjoying the views of the surrounding mountains.
Local Bakeries: Visit local bakeries for reasonably priced sandwiches and pastries. It's a cost-effective way to fuel up before your outdoor adventures.

- **Aare River Walk:** Take a leisurely walk along the Aare River for free. Enjoy the scenic beauty and the serene atmosphere of Interlaken's riverfront.
- **Höhematte Park Relaxation:** Unwind in Höhematte Park, a large green space in the center of Interlaken. Enjoy a picnic or simply relax and take in the mountain views for free.
- **Interlaken Casino Visit:** Experience the thrill of the Interlaken Casino for around 10 CHF. Enjoy an evening of entertainment and gaming.
- **Harder Kulm Funicular Ride:** Take the funicular to Harder Kulm for panoramic views of Interlaken and the surrounding mountains. The round-trip ticket is approximately 38 CHF.
- **Boat Cruise on Lake Thun or Lake Brienz:** Embark on a boat cruise on Lake Thun or Lake Brienz for around 30 CHF. Revel in the breathtaking scenery as you cruise along the pristine lakes.
- **Heimwehfluh Funicular and Miniature Park:** Ride the funicular to Heimwehfluh for about 18 CHF. Explore the Miniature Park and enjoy stunning views of Interlaken.
- **Interlaken Walking Tour:** Join a guided walking tour of Interlaken for around 20-30 CHF. Learn about the town's history, landmarks, and cultural highlights.
- **Swiss Open-Air Museum Ballenberg:** Visit the Swiss Open-Air Museum Ballenberg for approximately 28 CHF. Explore traditional Swiss architecture and culture in a beautiful outdoor setting.

Trümmelbach Falls Visit: Discover the Trümmelbach Falls, accessible by public transport, for around 13 CHF. Marvel at the cascading waterfalls inside the mountain.
Schynige Platte Railway Journey: Take the cogwheel railway to Schynige Platte for approximately 62 CHF. Enjoy panoramic views of the Eiger, Mönch, and Jungfrau.
Adventure Park Interlaken: Experience the Adventure Park Interlaken for around 65 CHF. Enjoy high ropes courses, zip lines, and other thrilling activities.
Interlaken West Beach: Relax at Interlaken West Beach for free. Enjoy the lakeside ambiance and soak in the stunning views of the surrounding mountains.
Alpenwildpark Interlaken: Explore the Alpenwildpark Interlaken for around 5 CHF. Encounter native Swiss wildlife in a natural setting.
Heimatwerk Interlaken Shopping: Explore Heimatwerk Interlaken for Swiss souvenirs and traditional crafts. While shopping may incur costs, browsing is free.
St. Beatus Caves Visit: Discover the St. Beatus Caves for around 22 CHF. Explore the underground cave system with impressive stalactite formations.
Interlaken Golf Club: Enjoy a round of golf at the Interlaken Golf Club. While it may not be budget-friendly, the lush course offers a luxurious sporting experience.
Interlaken Horse Carriage Ride: Take a horse carriage ride around Interlaken for approximately 45 CHF. Enjoy a relaxing tour with a touch of old-world charm.
Grindelwald Day Trip: Take a day trip to Grindelwald for about 25 CHF. Explore the alpine village and enjoy stunning views of the Eiger.
Sailing on Lake Thun or Lake Brienz: Experience sailing on Lake Thun or Lake Brienz for around 60 CHF. Enjoy the tranquility of the lakes and the surrounding mountains.
Giessbach Falls Boat and Funicular: Visit Giessbach Falls and take the boat and funicular for approximately 20 CHF. Marvel at the cascading falls and enjoy the scenic journey.

Aspect	Money saving tips
Accommodation	Consider budget-friendly hotels like Hotel Beausite, hostels such as Balmers Hostel, or explore affordable options on booking platforms.
Transportation	Use the Interlaken Visitor Card for free local transportation, explore the town on foot, and consider renting a bike for a cost-effective option.
Dining	Enjoy budget-friendly options at Hüsi Bierhaus for Swiss cuisine, cafes like Cafe de la Poste, and affordable eateries like Restaurant Chalet.
Sightseeing	Utilize the Interlaken Visitor Card for discounts on boat rides, cable cars, and local attractions. Explore the Höhematte Park and Aare River promenade independently.
Entertainment	Take advantage of free outdoor activities like hiking and enjoy the scenic beauty of Lake Thun and Lake Brienz.
Shopping	Explore budget-friendly shopping at Hoheweg Promenade and Interlaken West Shopping Center for souvenirs and Swiss chocolates.
Day Trips	Plan a cost-effective day trip to Lauterbrunnen Valley or Grindelwald using the efficient Swiss public transportation system.
Currency Exchange	Withdraw local currency from ATMs for better rates, avoid high fees by using local banks.
Timing	Visit during the shoulder seasons (spring or fall) for pleasant weather and potentially lower prices.

| Technology | Use budget-friendly apps like Interlaken Official Guide for information, Maps.me for navigation, and local deal apps for discounts. |

Zermatt

Situated in the Valais canton of Switzerland, Zermatt is renowned for its breathtaking Alpine scenery and serves as a gateway to some of the most spectacular peaks in the Swiss Alps. Zermatt underwent a transformation in the mid-19th century when it became a popular destination for mountaineers. The ascent of the Matterhorn in 1865, albeit tragic, brought international attention to Zermatt and solidified its status as a premier alpine resort. The Gornergrat Railway, one of the world's first cogwheel railways, opened in 1898, enhancing accessibility to the high-altitude panoramas. Zermatt is car-free, with electric taxis and horse-drawn carriages navigating its charming streets. Today, it is a haven for outdoor enthusiasts, offering world-class skiing, hiking, and mountaineering experiences. The village, surrounded by towering peaks, retains its alpine charm and stands as a testament to the harmonious coexistence of human settlement and majestic natural beauty.

1. Affordable Accommodation:

Budget-Friendly Guesthouses: Consider staying in guesthouses like Hotel Alfa Zermatt or Hotel Rhodania for a more affordable yet comfortable experience in the heart of Zermatt.
Hostels with Views: Zermatt has hostels like Zermatt Youth Hostel offering budget accommodations with stunning views of the Matterhorn.

2. Cheap Eats:

Street Food and Takeaways: Explore the Bahnhofstrasse area for affordable street food and takeaways. Local eateries offer delicious options without breaking the bank.
Grocery Stores: Save on meals by grabbing fresh produce and snacks from local grocery stores. Enjoy a picnic with a view of the Matterhorn.

Luxury for less

    Gornergrat Railway Excursion: Take the Gornergrat Railway for panoramic views of the Matterhorn and the surrounding Alps. The round-trip ticket is approximately 90 CHF.
    Matterhorn Museum Visit: Explore the Matterhorn Museum for around 10 CHF. Discover the history of Zermatt and the stories of mountaineering.
    Hiking Trails: Explore Zermatt's hiking trails for free. Enjoy the breathtaking scenery of the Alps at your own pace.

Schwarzsee (Black Lake) Hike: Take a hike to Schwarzsee for free. Enjoy the serenity and stunning views of the Matterhorn along the way.

Gornergrat Trail: Hike the Gornergrat Trail for free. Experience breathtaking vistas of the Matterhorn and surrounding peaks.

Zermatt Walk of Climb: Embark on the Zermatt Walk of Climb for free. Discover the history of mountaineering and climbing in the region.

Gorner Gorge Visit: Explore the Gorner Gorge for around 6 CHF. Traverse wooden walkways and witness the power of glacial waters.

Zermatt Ice Pavilion: Visit the Zermatt Ice Pavilion for around 10 CHF. Explore ice caves and tunnels within the Gorner Glacier.

Stellisee Lake Reflections: Hike to Stellisee Lake for free. Capture stunning reflections of the Matterhorn in the pristine alpine waters.

Skiing in Zermatt: While skiing can be a significant expense, Zermatt offers a world-class skiing experience. Prices for lift passes vary depending on the duration.

Zermatt Village Stroll: Take a leisurely stroll through the charming car-free village of Zermatt for free. Enjoy its quaint streets, shops, and alpine ambiance.

Zermatt-Furi Cable Car: Take the cable car to Furi for approximately 45 CHF. Enjoy the scenic ride and access to hiking trails.

Sunnegga Paradise Visit: Explore Sunnegga Paradise for around 70 CHF. Enjoy breathtaking views of the Matterhorn and the surrounding peaks.

Gourmet Dining in Zermatt: Indulge in a gourmet dining experience at one of Zermatt's renowned restaurants. While it may not be budget-friendly, the culinary experience is luxurious.

Gornergrat Observatory: Visit the Gornergrat Observatory for around 35 CHF. Observe the night sky and the Matterhorn in all its glory.

Zermatt Cheese Factory: Explore a Zermatt cheese factory for free. Learn about traditional Swiss cheese-making processes.

Heli-Skiing Adventure: For those seeking an adventurous luxury experience, consider heli-skiing in the Zermatt region. Prices vary based on the package and location.

Paragliding over Zermatt: Soar above Zermatt with a paragliding experience for around 160 CHF. Enjoy breathtaking aerial views of the Alps.

Cervinia Day Trip: Take a day trip to Cervinia in Italy for around 90 CHF. Experience the Italian Alps and enjoy skiing or hiking.

Aspect	Money saving tips
Accommodation	Consider budget-friendly hotels like Hotel Alfa Zermatt, hostels such as Matterhorn Hostel, or explore affordable options on booking platforms.
Transportation	Use the Gornergrat Bahn for budget-friendly travel to viewpoints, explore the village on foot, and consider the Zermatt Visitor Card for local transportation discounts.
Dining	Enjoy budget-friendly options at places like Brown Cow Pub for casual dining, cafes such as Café du Pont, and affordable eateries like Restaurant Du Pont for Swiss dishes.
Sightseeing	Explore the village on foot and take advantage of free viewpoints like Gornergrat Railway Station. Consider budget-friendly cable car rides like Sunnegga and Hiking trails.

Entertainment	Enjoy free outdoor activities like hiking, and take in the breathtaking views of the Matterhorn.
Shopping	Explore budget-friendly shopping at the Bahnhofstrasse and Zermatt Handwerk for souvenirs and Swiss products.
Day Trips	Plan a cost-effective day trip to Gornergrat or Schwarzsee using the efficient Swiss public transportation system.
Currency Exchange	Withdraw local currency from ATMs for better rates, avoid high fees by using local banks.
Timing	Visit during the shoulder seasons (spring or fall) for pleasant weather and potentially lower prices.
Technology	Use budget-friendly apps like Zermatt Tourism for information, Maps.me for navigation, and local deal apps for discounts.

Lausanne

Lausanne, situated on the shores of Lake Geneva and surrounded by vineyards, is known for its cultural richness and picturesque landscapes.

Originally a Roman settlement, Lausanne evolved over the centuries into a major center for trade and commerce. In the medieval era, it became a Bishopric, and the impressive Lausanne Cathedral, dating back to the 12th century, stands as a testament to this period. The city played a pivotal role in the Protestant Reformation, with figures like John Calvin leaving their mark. Lausanne became a hub for education and culture, hosting the University of Lausanne (UNIL) and the Swiss Federal Institute of Technology in Lausanne (EPFL).

Lausanne's dedication to the Olympic Movement is underscored by the presence of the International Olympic Committee (IOC) headquarters since 1915. The city's vibrant cultural scene is further enhanced by theaters, museums, and the renowned Collection de l'Art Brut. Lausanne's lakeside setting, combined with its historic Old Town and the evolving Flon district, creates a captivating blend of tradition and modernity. Today, Lausanne stands as a dynamic city known for its international influence, cultural richness, and its role as the Olympic capital.

1. Affordable Accommodation:

Budget-Friendly Hotels: Consider staying at hotels like Hotel Lausanne by Fassbind or Hotel Aulac for a cost-effective yet comfortable stay in Lausanne.
Hostels with Style: Lausanne offers hostels like Lausanne Youth Hostel, providing budget-friendly accommodation with a modern touch.

2. Cheap Eats:

Food Markets: Visit local markets like Lausanne-Moudon Market for fresh and affordable produce. Grab some Swiss cheese, bread, and fruits for a budget-friendly picnic by Lake Geneva.
Ethnic Eateries in Flon District: Explore the Flon district for budget-friendly ethnic restaurants and cafes offering diverse and delicious options.

3. Luxury for less

- **Olympic Museum Visit:** Explore the Olympic Museum for around 18 CHF. Immerse yourself in the history of the Olympic Games and experience interactive exhibits.
- **Lausanne Cathedral Climb:** Ascend the Lausanne Cathedral Tower for panoramic views of the city and Lake Geneva. The entrance fee is approximately 5 CHF.
- **Collection de l'Art Brut:** Discover the Collection de l'Art Brut for around 18 CHF. Explore an extraordinary collection of outsider art.
- **Ouchy Promenade:** Take a leisurely stroll along the Ouchy Promenade for free. Enjoy views of Lake Geneva and the Alps, with the option to relax by the lakeside.
- **Hermitage Foundation Museum:** Visit the Hermitage Foundation Museum for around 18 CHF. Admire a collection of fine arts and decorative arts in a beautiful setting.
- **Esplanade de Montbenon:** Relax at the Esplanade de Montbenon for free. Enjoy the green space, sculptures, and views of the surrounding area.
- **Lausanne City Walking Tour:** Join a guided walking tour of Lausanne for around 20-30 CHF. Explore the Old Town, learn about local history, and visit cultural landmarks.
- **Parc de Mon Repos:** Enjoy Parc de Mon Repos for free. This park offers a peaceful retreat with gardens, a pond, and sculptures.
- **Musée de l'Elysée:** Explore the Musée de l'Elysée for around 25 CHF. Discover photography exhibitions in this renowned museum.
- **Lausanne Vineyard Tour:** Take a self-guided or organized vineyard tour in the Lavaux region. Enjoy stunning views of Lake Geneva and the vine-covered hills.
- **Rolex Learning Center:** Visit the Rolex Learning Center at EPFL for free. Admire the futuristic architecture and innovative design.
- **Lutry Lakeside Walk:** Explore the lakeside town of Lutry for free. Wander along the shores of Lake Geneva, visit the medieval town center, and enjoy lakeside cafes.
- **Pully Lakeside Park:** Relax in Pully Lakeside Park for free. Enjoy the peaceful ambiance and views of the lake and mountains.
- **Cantonal Museum of Fine Arts (Musée cantonal des Beaux-Arts):** Discover the Cantonal Museum of Fine Arts for around 10 CHF. Explore a diverse collection of Swiss and international art.
- **Lausanne Botanical Garden:** Explore the Lausanne Botanical Garden for around 6 CHF. Wander through themed gardens and enjoy the tranquility.
- **Rochers-de-Naye Day Trip:** Take a day trip to Rochers-de-Naye for approximately 74 CHF. Enjoy a scenic train ride and panoramic views of the Alps.
- **Lausanne Opera House Performance:** Attend a performance at the Lausanne Opera House. Ticket prices vary, but affordable options may be available for around 30 CHF.
- **Vallée de la Jeunesse Park:** Enjoy Vallée de la Jeunesse Park for free. This park offers green spaces, a lake, and a playground.
- **Lausanne History Museum:** Explore the Lausanne History Museum for around 8 CHF. Learn about the history of Lausanne and its cultural heritage.
- **Lavaux Wine Tasting:** Experience wine tasting in the Lavaux vineyards. Prices vary, but you can find budget-friendly options for sampling local wines.

4. Cultural Events:

Free Museum Days: Take advantage of free entry days at museums like the Collection de l'Art Brut or the Olympic Museum. Many museums offer free access on specific days or during certain hours.
Street Performances in Flon: Explore the Flon district for street performances and artistic displays. The area often hosts cultural events that are free to attend.

5. Budget-Friendly Transport:

Lausanne Transport Card: Some accommodations provide guests with a Lausanne Transport Card, offering free access to public transportation within the city. Utilize buses and metro services to explore without extra expenses.
Walking Tour of Old Town: Discover the charm of Lausanne's Old Town on foot. Wander through cobbled streets and explore historic landmarks like the Lausanne Cathedral at your own pace.

By blending these budget-friendly tips, you can experience the cultural richness and scenic beauty of Lausanne without exceeding your budget, making your visit both affordable and enjoyable.

Aspect	Money saving tips
Accommodation	Consider budget-friendly hotels like ibis Lausanne Centre, hostels such as Lausanne Guesthouse & Backpacker, or explore affordable options on booking platforms.
Transportation	Use Lausanne Transport Card for free local transportation, explore the city on foot, and consider renting a bike for a cost-effective option.
Dining	Enjoy budget-friendly options at places like Holy Cow! Gourmet Burger Company, cafes such as Le Barbare, and affordable eateries like La Croix d'Ouchy for Swiss cuisine.
Sightseeing	Visit free attractions like Olympic Museum Gardens, stroll around Ouchy Promenade and explore the Old Town (Cité). Take advantage of the Lausanne Transport Card for discounts on local attractions.
Entertainment	Attend free events at Place de la Riponne, relax by Lake Geneva, or explore the Collection de l'Art Brut.
Shopping	Explore budget-friendly shopping at Rue de Bourg and Lausanne Flea Market for unique finds and souvenirs.
Day Trips	Plan a cost-effective day trip to Montreux or Vevey using the efficient Swiss public transportation system.
Currency Exchange	Withdraw local currency from ATMs for better rates, avoid high fees by using local banks.
Timing	Visit during the shoulder seasons (spring or fall) for pleasant weather and potentially lower prices.
Technology	Use budget-friendly apps like Mobilis Lausanne for public transportation, Maps.me for navigation, and local deal apps for discounts.

Basel

Basel is a vibrant and culturally rich city in northwestern Switzerland. This cosmopolitan hub, straddling the borders of Switzerland, Germany, and France, showcases a unique blend of history, modernity, and artistic expression.

Founded by the Romans around the 1st century BC, Basel has evolved into a major economic and cultural hub. The city's Old Town, with its medieval architecture, narrow cobblestone streets, and landmarks like the Basel Minster, reflects its historical significance.

Basel has long been a center for trade and commerce, strategically positioned at the crossroads of Switzerland, France, and Germany. The Rhine River, flowing through the city, has played a crucial role in its development. The University of Basel, established in 1460, is one of the oldest universities in Switzerland and has contributed significantly to the city's intellectual and cultural legacy.

The Kunstmuseum Basel, Fondation Beyeler, and the Tinguely Museum are just a few examples of Basel's thriving art scene. The city hosts Art Basel, one of the world's premier contemporary art fairs. Basel also boasts a dynamic culinary scene, vibrant markets, and an array of festivals throughout the year.

As a major cultural and economic center, Basel is home to numerous international organizations, including the headquarters of major pharmaceutical companies.

1. Affordable Accommodation:

Budget-Friendly Hotels: Consider staying at hotels like Hotel Rochat or Hotel Alexander for affordable yet comfortable accommodation in Basel.
Hostels with Character: Basel offers hostels like Basel Backpack, providing budget-friendly stays with a vibrant atmosphere.

2. Cheap Eats:

Markthalle Basel: Explore Markthalle Basel, a bustling market with diverse food stalls offering affordable and delicious international cuisine.
Rhine Riverbank: Enjoy budget-friendly snacks along the Rhine Riverbank. Grab a pastry or a sandwich and have a riverside picnic with a view.

3. Luxury for less

- **Kunstmuseum Basel:** Explore Kunstmuseum Basel for around 20 CHF. Admire an impressive collection of Swiss, German, and French art from the Middle Ages to contemporary works.
- **Basel Minster Tower Climb:** Ascend the Basel Minster Tower for panoramic views of the city and the Rhine River. The entrance fee is approximately 5 CHF.
- **Tinguely Museum Visit:** Discover the Tinguely Museum for around 18 CHF. Explore the fascinating world of Swiss artist Jean Tinguely's kinetic art.
- **Rhine River Walk:** Take a leisurely walk along the Rhine River for free. Enjoy the scenic views of the river and the city.
- **Basel Zoo Visit:** Visit Basel Zoo for approximately 30 CHF. Explore a variety of exhibits and enjoy encounters with animals from around the world.
- **Swiss Architecture Museum:** Explore the Swiss Architecture Museum for around 12 CHF. Delve into the world of architecture through exhibitions and installations.
- **Old Town Basel Exploration:** Wander through the charming Old Town of Basel for free. Explore narrow streets, visit historic squares, and admire medieval architecture.
- **Botanical Garden of the University of Basel:** Explore the Botanical Garden for around 5 CHF. Enjoy a diverse collection of plants and themed gardens.
- **Kunsthalle Basel:** Discover Kunsthalle Basel for around 12 CHF. Experience contemporary art exhibitions in this dynamic art space.
- **Fondation Beyeler Day Trip:** Take a day trip to the Fondation Beyeler for around 35 CHF. Explore this renowned art museum located in a beautiful park setting near Basel.
- **Basel Historical Museum:** Visit the Basel Historical Museum for around 10 CHF. Explore exhibits on cultural history, archaeology, and applied arts.
- **Augusta Raurica Day Trip:** Take a day trip to Augusta Raurica, a Roman archaeological site near Basel, for approximately 14 CHF. Explore ancient ruins and a museum.
- **Dreiländereck (Three Countries Corner):** Visit Dreiländereck, where Switzerland, Germany, and France meet, for free. Enjoy the unique experience of standing in three countries at once.
- **Kunsthaus Baselland:** Explore Kunsthaus Baselland for around 10 CHF. This contemporary art space showcases a variety of exhibitions.
- **Rheinbad Swimming in the Rhine:** Experience swimming in the Rhine River at Rheinbad for around 1-2 CHF. Join the locals in this unique summer activity.
- **Herzog & de Meuron Walking Tour:** Take a self-guided walking tour to explore buildings designed by Herzog & de Meuron, the renowned Swiss architecture firm. This is a free activity.
- **Fasnacht Fountain Tour:** Explore Basel's fountains, each uniquely decorated during the Fasnacht (Carnival) season. This is a free and festive activity.
- **Paper Mill Museum:** Visit the Paper Mill Museum for around 6 CHF. Learn about the history of paper production in a fascinating museum setting.

- **Museum Tinguely Fountain:** Admire the Jean Tinguely Fountain near Theaterplatz for free. This kinetic sculpture in the heart of the city is a Basel landmark.
- **Lange Erlen Park:** Enjoy Lange Erlen Park for free. This park offers green spaces, a playground, and a petting zoo, providing a relaxing escape.

4. Cultural Events:

Kunstmuseum Basel: Visit the Kunstmuseum Basel on Thursdays, as entry is free during the evening hours. Explore a rich collection of art without any cost.
Outdoor Performances: Keep an eye out for free outdoor performances and cultural events happening in public spaces or parks, especially during the summer months.

5. Budget-Friendly Transport:

Basel Card: Many hotels provide guests with a Basel Card, offering free use of public transportation within the city. Use trams and buses to explore Basel conveniently without additional expenses.
Biking in Basel: Rent a bike and explore the city on two wheels. Basel is bike-friendly, and it's an affordable and eco-friendly way to see the sights.
By combining these budget-friendly tips, you can immerse yourself in Basel's cultural scene, enjoy its scenic landscapes, and explore its history without straining your budget, making your visit both economical and delightful.

Aspect	Money saving tips
Accommodation	Consider budget-friendly hotels like Hotel Rochat, hostels such as Basel Backpack, or explore affordable options on booking platforms.
Transportation	Use the Basel Card for free local transportation, explore the city on foot, and consider using trams for efficient and affordable travel.
Dining	Enjoy budget-friendly options at places like Markthalle Basel for diverse food options, cafes such as Café Frühling, and affordable eateries like Restaurant Fischerstube for Swiss dishes.
Sightseeing	Visit free attractions like Basel Minster Square, explore the Old Town (Altstadt), and take advantage of the Basel Card for discounts on museums and attractions.
Entertainment	Attend free events in Münsterplatz, relax by the Rhine River, or explore Kunsthalle Basel for contemporary art.
Shopping	Explore budget-friendly shopping at Freie Strasse and Basel's flea markets for unique finds and affordable souvenirs.
Day Trips	Plan a cost-effective day trip to Rhine Falls or the Black Forest using the efficient Swiss public transportation system.
Currency Exchange	Withdraw local currency from ATMs for better rates, avoid high fees by using local banks.
Timing	Visit during the shoulder seasons (spring or fall) for pleasant weather and potentially lower prices.
Technology	Use budget-friendly apps like BLT Mobile for public transportation, Maps.me for navigation, and local deal apps for discounts.

Montreux

in the French-speaking part of Switzerland, Montreux is a picturesque town renowned for its stunning lakeside setting, mild climate, and its annual jazz festival. This charming destination, embraced by vineyards and surrounded by the Swiss Alps, offers a unique blend of natural beauty and cultural vibrancy.

The city has a history dating back to the medieval period when a fortress was built to guard the strategically important trade route along Lake Geneva.

Montreux gained prominence in the 19th century as a favored destination for European aristocracy seeking the healing properties of its climate. The opening of the Montreux-Oberland Bernois Railway in 1900 further facilitated tourism, connecting Montreux to the surrounding mountain regions.

One of the most iconic events associated with Montreux is the Montreux Jazz Festival, founded in 1967. This globally acclaimed music festival has welcomed legendary artists and continues to draw music enthusiasts from around the world.

The city is also celebrated for its picturesque lakeside promenade, flower-filled parks, and the Chillon Castle, situated on a small island in Lake Geneva. The annual Christmas market and the Rochers-de-Naye cogwheel railway, offering panoramic views, are additional highlights.

Montreux's association with creativity and natural beauty, as well as its strategic location along the Swiss Riviera, has solidified its reputation as a captivating destination for both leisure and cultural experiences.

1. Affordable Accommodation:

Budget-Friendly Hotels: Consider staying at hotels like Hotel Helvetie or Tralala Hotel Montreux for affordable and cozy accommodation with a touch of Swiss charm.
Guesthouses by Lake Geneva: Explore guesthouses in the vicinity of Lake Geneva, offering budget-friendly stays with beautiful lake views.

2. Cheap Eats:

Lakeside Picnic: Grab fresh produce from local markets or grocery stores and enjoy a budget-friendly picnic by the shores of Lake Geneva. Take in the stunning views of the Alps and the lake.
Market Street Eateries: Stroll through Montreux's market streets for affordable eateries offering Swiss and international cuisine. Enjoy a meal without breaking the bank.

3. Luxury for less

- **Chillon Castle Visit:** Explore Chillon Castle for around 13 CHF. Discover medieval architecture and enjoy views of Lake Geneva.

- **Montreux Jazz Festival (During the Festival):** Attend the Montreux Jazz Festival for a unique musical experience. Ticket prices vary based on the performers and the type of event.
- **Rochers-de-Naye Day Trip:** Take a day trip to Rochers-de-Naye for approximately 74 CHF. Enjoy a scenic train ride and panoramic views of Lake Geneva and the Alps.
- **Montreux Lakeside Promenade:** Take a leisurely walk along the Montreux Lakeside Promenade for free. Enjoy the views of the lake, mountains, and flower-filled promenade.
- **Freddy Mercury Statue:** Visit the Freddy Mercury Statue on the lakeside promenade for free. Pay homage to the legendary Queen singer who lived in Montreux.
- **Montreux Music & Convention Center (2m2c):** Attend cultural events and concerts at 2m2c. Ticket prices vary, with options for different budgets.
- **Montreux Jazz Café:** Enjoy a meal or drinks at the Montreux Jazz Café. While dining may incur costs, the ambiance and occasional live music create a luxurious experience.
- **Territet-Glion Funicular:** Take the Territet-Glion Funicular for approximately 25 CHF. Enjoy the scenic ride and breathtaking views of Lake Geneva.
- **Ride on the Rochers-de-Naye Cogwheel Train:** Experience the cogwheel train to Rochers-de-Naye for around 74 CHF. Revel in panoramic views and visit the marmot park.
- **Lavaux Vineyard Terraces Day Trip:** Take a day trip to the Lavaux Vineyard Terraces for approximately 30 CHF. Explore the UNESCO-listed vineyards and enjoy wine tasting.
- **Montreux Christmas Market (During the Season):** Explore the Montreux Christmas Market for free. Experience festive decorations, local crafts, and seasonal treats.
- **Swiss National Audiovisual Museum (Médiathèque Valais):** Visit the Swiss National Audiovisual Museum for around 15 CHF. Explore audiovisual archives and exhibits.
- **Signal de Bougy Park:** Enjoy Signal de Bougy Park for around 5 CHF. This family-friendly park offers a variety of activities, including a mini-zoo.
- **Territet to Glion Hiking Trail:** Hike the trail from Territet to Glion for free. Experience stunning views of Lake Geneva and the surrounding mountains.
- **Montreux Art Gallery:** Visit the Montreux Art Gallery for around 20 CHF. Explore contemporary art exhibitions in a vibrant gallery setting.
- **Golf at Montreux Golf Club:** Enjoy a round of golf at Montreux Golf Club. While it may not be budget-friendly, the lush course offers a luxurious sporting experience.
- **Montreux Chocolate Train:** Experience the Montreux Chocolate Train for approximately 79 CHF. Indulge in Swiss chocolate tastings and explore Gruyères and Broc.
- **Montreux Casino:** Visit Montreux Casino for free. While gaming may incur costs, exploring the iconic casino and its surroundings is an atmospheric experience.
- **Lavaux Panoramic Wine Tour:** Take a panoramic wine tour in Lavaux for approximately 50 CHF. Enjoy a guided tour of the vineyards with wine tasting.
- **Parc Vernex:** Enjoy Parc Vernex for free. This park offers a tranquil space with green lawns and views of the surrounding area.

4. Cultural Events:

Montreux Jazz Festival Free Stages: If visiting during the Montreux Jazz Festival, enjoy free performances at various stages throughout the city. Immerse yourself in the musical atmosphere without purchasing tickets.

Art Exhibitions at Montreux Art Gallery: Check for free art exhibitions at venues like the Montreux Art Gallery, offering a cultural experience without an entry fee.

5. Budget-Friendly Transport:

Montreux Transport Card: Some accommodations provide guests with a Montreux Transport Card, offering free or discounted use of local public transportation. Use buses or boats to explore nearby areas without extra expenses.

Walk along Rochers-de-Naye Railway: Skip the train ride and take a scenic walk along the Rochers-de-Naye Railway trail. Enjoy the stunning views of Lake Geneva and the mountains without paying for the train ticket.

By incorporating these budget-friendly tips, you can relish the beauty of Montreux, experience its cultural offerings, and enjoy the serene ambiance of Lake Geneva without straining your budget, making your visit both economical and memorable.

Aspect	Money saving tips
Accommodation	Consider budget-friendly hotels like Hotel Helvetie, hostels such as Montreux Jazz Hostel, or explore affordable options on booking platforms.
Transportation	Use the Montreux Riviera Card for free local transportation, explore the lakeside promenade on foot, and consider the Swiss Travel Pass for discounted regional travel.
Dining	Enjoy budget-friendly options at places like Le Comptoir, cafes such as Montreux Jazz Café, and affordable eateries like Café-Restaurant Le National for Swiss cuisine.
Sightseeing	Stroll along the lakeside promenade, visit the free Rochers-de-Naye viewpoint, and explore Chillon Castle with the Montreux Riviera Card for discounts.
Entertainment	Attend free events at Montreux Jazz Festival (if during the festival), relax by Lake Geneva, or explore the Montreux Jazz Café for live music.
Shopping	Explore budget-friendly shopping at Grand Rue and Montreux Christmas Market (if visiting during the season) for unique finds and souvenirs.
Day Trips	Plan a cost-effective day trip to Gruyères or Vevey using the efficient Swiss public transportation system.
Currency Exchange	Withdraw local currency from ATMs for better rates, avoid high fees by using local banks.
Timing	Visit during the shoulder seasons (spring or fall) for pleasant weather and potentially lower prices.
Technology	Use budget-friendly apps like SBB Mobile for transportation, Maps.me for navigation, and local deal apps for discounts.

Grindelwald

Eiger

Grindelwald is a captivating Alpine village that enchants visitors with its breathtaking mountain landscapes, charming chalets, and outdoor recreational opportunities. Surrounded by the iconic Eiger, Mönch, and Jungfrau peaks, Grindelwald is a haven for nature lovers and adventure seekers. The village itself exudes alpine charm with its wooden chalets, flower-adorned balconies, and a backdrop of snow-capped mountains. The Eiger village, a part of Grindelwald, is particularly famous for its close-up views of the Eiger's notorious north face.

1. Affordable Accommodation:

Budget-Friendly Hostels: Grindelwald offers hostels like Mountain Hostel Grindelwald or Eiger Guesthouse, providing budget-friendly stays with a cozy mountain atmosphere.
Guesthouses in Wengen: Explore nearby Wengen for affordable guesthouses. The short train ride from Grindelwald to Wengen offers budget-friendly accommodation options with stunning mountain views.

2. Cheap Eats:

Self-Catering Picnic: Visit local grocery stores and bakeries for fresh produce and snacks. Enjoy a budget-friendly picnic with a view of the iconic Eiger, Mönch, and Jungfrau mountains.

Alpine Hut Cuisine: Explore mountain huts for affordable Alpine cuisine. Many huts offer hearty meals that won't break the bank.

3. Luxury for less

- **First Flyer Zip Line:** Experience the First Flyer Zip Line for around 40 CHF. Soar over the alpine landscapes for an exhilarating adventure.
- **Hike to Bachalpsee:** Hike to the stunning Bachalpsee for free. Enjoy the breathtaking reflections of the surrounding mountains in this alpine lake.
- **Jungfraujoch Day Trip:** Take a day trip to Jungfraujoch, the "Top of Europe," for around 120 CHF. Experience panoramic views and visit the Ice Palace.
- **Grindelwald First Cable Car:** Ride the Grindelwald First Cable Car for approximately 60 CHF. Enjoy scenic views as you ascend to the First summit.
- **Hike to Eiger Trail:** Hike the Eiger Trail for free. Experience close-up views of the Eiger North Face and the surrounding peaks.
- **Grindelwald-Männlichen Gondola Ride:** Take the gondola to Männlichen for around 40 CHF. Enjoy spectacular views of the Jungfrau, Mönch, and Eiger mountains.
- **Skiing in Grindelwald:** Experience skiing in Grindelwald during the winter season. Prices for lift passes and equipment rentals vary.
- **Hike to Kleine Scheidegg:** Hike to Kleine Scheidegg for free. Enjoy breathtaking views of the surrounding mountains and the Jungfraujoch.
- **Swiss Mountain Market:** Explore the Swiss Mountain Market for free. Experience local crafts, food, and traditional Swiss culture.
- **First Cliff Walk:** Walk the First Cliff Walk for around 38 CHF. Admire stunning views of the Eiger and surrounding peaks from this suspended walkway.
- **Männlichen Royal Walk:** Take the Royal Walk at Männlichen for approximately 20 CHF. Enjoy panoramic views and interactive installations.
- **Grindelwald Hike to Wengen:** Hike from Grindelwald to Wengen for free. Experience the beauty of the Swiss Alps along this scenic trail.
- **Gletscherschlucht Grindelwald (Glacier Gorge):** Explore the Glacier Gorge for around 12 CHF. Walk through narrow paths and witness the power of glacial waters.
- **First Flyer at Night:** Experience the First Flyer at night for approximately 65 CHF. Soar through the alpine landscape under the starry sky.
- **Hike to Faulhorn:** Hike to Faulhorn for free. Enjoy panoramic views of the Alps and the surrounding lakes.
- **Grindelwald Museum:** Explore the Grindelwald Museum for around 5 CHF. Learn about the history and culture of this alpine village.
- **Schynige Platte Railway Journey:** Take the Schynige Platte Railway for around 38 CHF. Enjoy scenic views of the Bernese Oberland.
- **First Glider Flight:** Experience the First Glider Flight for around 75 CHF. Soar through the air with stunning views of the Swiss Alps.
- **Hike to the Top of Pfingstegg:** Hike to the top of Pfingstegg for free. Enjoy panoramic views of Grindelwald and the surrounding peaks.
- **Local Swiss Cuisine at Grindelwald Restaurants:** Indulge in local Swiss cuisine at Grindelwald restaurants. While dining may incur costs, savoring Swiss specialties is a luxurious experience.

4. Cultural Events:

Local Festivals: Check for local festivals and events happening in Grindelwald. Experience the rich Alpine culture through free events such as traditional music performances and folklore displays.

Nature Interpretation Center: Visit the Grindelwald Nature Interpretation Center for information about the region's flora and fauna. Entry is often free, providing an educational and cultural experience.

5. Budget-Friendly Transport:

Grindelwald Guest Card: Some accommodations offer a Grindelwald Guest Card, providing free or discounted use of local buses and trains. Use this card to explore the surrounding areas without additional expenses.

Walk or Bike: Grindelwald is a pedestrian-friendly village. Explore on foot or rent a bike for an affordable and eco-friendly way to enjoy the scenery.

By combining these budget-friendly tips, you can immerse yourself in the natural beauty of Grindelwald, experience the Alpine culture, and explore the majestic mountains without exceeding your budget, making your visit both economical and enchanting.

Aspect	Money saving tips
Accommodation	Consider budget-friendly hotels like Hotel Lauberhorn, hostels such as Eiger Guesthouse, or explore affordable options on booking platforms.
Transportation	Use the Grindelwald Guest Card for free local transportation, explore the village on foot, and consider the Jungfrau Travel Pass for discounted regional travel.
Dining	Enjoy budget-friendly options at places like Onkel Tom's Hütte, cafes such as Avocado Bar, and affordable eateries like Restaurant Central for Swiss specialties.
Sightseeing	Explore the village on foot, visit the First Flyer viewpoint, and take advantage of the Grindelwald Guest Card for discounts on cable cars and local attractions.
Entertainment	Hike the Eiger Trail for free outdoor recreation, enjoy the natural beauty of the Jungfrau region, and explore the local culture in Grindelwald.
Shopping	Explore budget-friendly shopping at the village center and local souvenir shops for unique finds.
Day Trips	Plan a cost-effective day trip to Wengen or Lauterbrunnen using the efficient Swiss public transportation system.
Currency Exchange	Withdraw local currency from ATMs for better rates, avoid high fees by using local banks.
Timing	Visit during the shoulder seasons (spring or fall) for pleasant weather and potentially lower prices. Winter is also a great time for budget travelers, as it's the off-season for hiking and skiing.
Technology	Use budget-friendly apps like Jungfrau Region Tourist Guide for information, Maps.me for navigation, and local deal apps for discounts.

Lugano

In the Italian-speaking canton of Ticino in southern Switzerland, Lugano is a captivating city that graces the shores of Lake Lugano. Renowned for its Mediterranean flair, Lugano combines Swiss efficiency with Italian charm, offering visitors a unique blend of cultural richness, scenic beauty, and a mild climate.

The city's history traces back to Roman times when it served as a vital center for trade and commerce. Lugano's Old Town, with its narrow cobblestone streets and charming squares, reflects its medieval origins. Over the centuries, Lugano evolved into a vibrant cultural and financial hub.

Lake Lugano, surrounded by lush hills and mountains, adds to the city's allure. Parco Ciani, a lakeside park, provides a tranquil escape, and the panoramic views from Monte Brè and Monte Generoso offer breathtaking perspectives of the region.

Lugano is celebrated for its cultural events, including the Lugano Arte e Cultura cultural center and the Lugano Festival. The city hosts international conferences and is a prominent banking and financial center, contributing to its cosmopolitan atmosphere.

With a blend of Swiss efficiency and Italian charm, Lugano invites visitors to enjoy its Mediterranean-style cafés, lakeside promenades, and a variety of outdoor activities. The city's unique cultural fusion makes it a captivating destination for those seeking a harmonious blend of Swiss and Italian influences.

1. Affordable Accommodation:

Budget-Friendly Hotels: Consider staying at hotels like Hotel Besso or Hotel Zurigo for affordable yet comfortable accommodations in Lugano.
Hostels and Guesthouses: Explore hostels and guesthouses in the city center or surrounding areas for budget-friendly stays with a local touch.

2. Cheap Eats:

Lakeside Picnic: Purchase fresh produce from local markets or grocery stores and enjoy a budget-friendly lakeside picnic. Lugano's lakeside parks offer scenic views of Lake Lugano and the surrounding mountains.
Street Food at Piazza della Riforma: Visit Piazza della Riforma for street food vendors offering a variety of affordable and delicious options.

3. Luxury for less

- **Parco Ciani (Ciani Park) Stroll:** Take a leisurely stroll in Parco Ciani for free. Enjoy the lush greenery and beautiful views of Lake Lugano.
- **Lugano Arte e Cultura (LAC) Concert:** Attend a concert or cultural event at LAC. Ticket prices vary, offering options for different budgets.
- **Monte Brè Funicular Ride:** Take the funicular to Monte Brè for around 23 CHF. Enjoy panoramic views of Lake Lugano and the surrounding mountains.

- **Parco Villa Ciani (Villa Ciani Park):** Explore Parco Villa Ciani for free. Wander through this historical park with sculptures, fountains, and a lakeside setting.
- **Lugano Arte e Cultura (LAC) Lakeside Walk:** Take a lakeside walk near LAC for free. Enjoy the views of the lake and the modern architectural design of LAC.
- **Swiss Miniature Village Visit:** Explore the Swiss Miniature Village for around 25 CHF. Experience a miniature Switzerland with replicas of famous landmarks.
- **Lugano Arte e Cultura (LAC) Rooftop Terrace:** Visit the rooftop terrace of LAC for free. Enjoy panoramic views of the city, Lake Lugano, and the surrounding hills.
- **Ostello Riposo Hostel Garden:** Relax in the garden of Ostello Riposo Hostel for free. This budget-friendly option provides a peaceful environment.
- **Lugano Città Vecchia (Old Town) Exploration:** Wander through Lugano's Old Town for free. Discover charming streets, historical buildings, and local shops.
- **Lugano Lakefront Promenade:** Take a leisurely stroll along the lakefront promenade for free. Admire the views of the lake and surrounding mountains.
- **Civico Museo d'Arte Moderna (Modern Art Museum):** Explore the Modern Art Museum for around 10 CHF. Discover contemporary Swiss and Italian artworks.
- **Parco San Grato Visit:** Take a day trip to Parco San Grato for around 8 CHF. Enjoy botanical gardens, sculptures, and views of Lake Lugano.
- **Lugano Cimitero Monumentale (Monumental Cemetery):** Visit the Monumental Cemetery for free. Admire impressive sculptures and peaceful surroundings.
- **Lugano Arte e Cultura (LAC) Outdoor Performances:** Attend free outdoor performances and events at LAC. Check the schedule for cultural offerings.
- **Swiss Customs Museum (Dogana Svizzera):** Explore the Swiss Customs Museum for around 10 CHF. Learn about the history of customs and smuggling in the region.
- **Lake Lugano Boat Cruise:** Enjoy a boat cruise on Lake Lugano for approximately 30 CHF. Experience the beauty of the lake and the surrounding hills.
- **Lugano Arte e Cultura (LAC) Open-Air Cinema:** Attend the open-air cinema at LAC. Ticket prices vary, offering a unique cinematic experience.
- **Cattedrale di San Lorenzo (Saint Lawrence Cathedral):** Visit the cathedral for free. Admire the architecture and enjoy a moment of tranquility.
- **Lugano Lido Beach:** Relax at Lugano Lido Beach for around 10 CHF. Enjoy the lakeside ambiance and swimming facilities.
- **Gandria Day Trip:** Take a boat or hike to the charming village of Gandria for approximately 20 CHF. Explore narrow streets and enjoy lake views.

4. Cultural Events:

Free Concerts at Parco Ciani: Check for free concerts and cultural events taking place at Parco Ciani, especially during the summer months. Enjoy music and performances in a picturesque setting.

Art Exhibitions at Lugano Arte e Cultura: Explore Lugano Arte e Cultura for free art exhibitions. Many cultural centers offer complimentary access to rotating displays.

5. Budget-Friendly Transport:

Lugano Card: Some accommodations provide guests with a Lugano Card, offering free or discounted use of public transportation within the city. Utilize buses and boats to explore Lugano conveniently without extra expenses.

Explore on Foot: Lugano is a walkable city with beautiful promenades and pedestrian-friendly areas. Discover the city's charm by exploring on foot, taking in the sights at your own pace.

By incorporating these budget-friendly tips, you can experience the beauty of Lugano, enjoy its cultural offerings, and relax by the lake without breaking the bank, making your visit both affordable and delightful.

Aspect	Money saving tips
Accommodation	Consider budget-friendly hotels like Hotel Federale Lugano, hostels such as Youth Hostel Lugano, or explore affordable options on booking platforms.
Transportation	Use the Ticino Ticket for free local transportation, explore the city on foot, and consider boat rides on Lake Lugano for a scenic and affordable experience.
Dining	Enjoy budget-friendly options at places like Gabbani for local cuisine, cafes such as Al Panino and affordable eateries like Trattoria Cacciatori.
Sightseeing	Explore the Parco Ciani and the Old Town (Centro Storico) on foot, visit Lugano Arte e Cultura for cultural events, and take advantage of the Ticino Ticket for discounts on local attractions.
Entertainment	Relax by Lake Lugano, attend free events in the city center, and explore Lugano's parks and public spaces.
Shopping	Explore budget-friendly shopping at Via Nassa and Mercato Coperto for souvenirs and local products.
Day Trips	Plan a cost-effective day trip to Morcote or Gandria using public boats or buses.
Currency Exchange	Withdraw local currency from ATMs for better rates, avoid high fees by using local banks.
Timing	Visit during the shoulder seasons (spring or fall) for pleasant weather and potentially lower prices.
Technology	Use budget-friendly apps like Trasporti Pubblici Luganesi for public transportation, Maps.me for navigation, and local deal apps for discounts.

St. Moritz

St. Moritz is a world-renowned resort town that epitomizes luxury, winter sports, and Alpine elegance. Famous for its glitzy ambiance, pristine landscapes, and hosting two Winter Olympics, St. Moritz has long been a playground for the elite and a symbol of Swiss sophistication.

St. Moritz has hosted the Winter Olympics twice (in 1928 and 1948) and is renowned for its world-class ski resorts, glamorous atmosphere, and upscale amenities. The town's pristine Lake St. Moritz becomes a winter playground, transforming into a frozen surface for activities such as polo and horse racing during the famed White Turf event.

The iconic Badrutt's Palace Hotel and other luxury accommodations contribute to St. Moritz's reputation as a playground for the affluent. The town also boasts high-end shopping, fine dining, and a vibrant cultural scene. Visitors can experience the spectacular Engadin landscape through activities like skiing, snowboarding, and hiking, while the surrounding mountains provide breathtaking panoramic views.

1. Affordable Accommodation:

Budget-Friendly Guesthouses: Consider staying in guesthouses or smaller hotels like Hotel Languard or Hotel Sonne for more budget-friendly options in St. Moritz.
Hostels in Nearby Towns: Explore hostels in nearby towns like Pontresina or Silvaplana, which can offer more affordable accommodation options with easy access to St. Moritz.

2. Cheap Eats:

Self-Catering Picnic: Purchase local cheese, bread, and fresh produce from markets like the Engadiner Wochenmarkt. Enjoy a budget-friendly picnic with stunning Alpine views.
Local Bakeries and Cafes: Visit local bakeries and cafes for reasonably priced snacks and pastries. Engadine specialties can be found at more affordable prices in local establishments.

3. Luxury for less

- **Corviglia Funicular Ride:** Take the funicular to Corviglia for approximately 30 CHF. Enjoy breathtaking views of the Engadin valley and surrounding peaks.

- **Lake St. Moritz Winter Walk:** Take a winter walk around Lake St. Moritz for free. Admire the frozen lake, snow-covered landscapes, and views of the town.
- **Muottas Muragl Railway Journey:** Take the Muottas Muragl funicular for around 38 CHF. Experience panoramic views of the Engadin valley and the Bernina Range.
- **Diavolezza Cable Car Ride:** Ride the Diavolezza Cable Car for approximately 74 CHF. Revel in stunning views of the Bernina Massif and the Morteratsch Glacier.
- **Cross-Country Skiing on the Engadin Trails:** Experience cross-country skiing on the Engadin trails. Prices for trail access and equipment rentals vary.
- **St. Moritz Bad Mineral Bath:** Relax in the St. Moritz Bad Mineral Bath for around 20 CHF. Enjoy the healing properties of the local mineral springs.
- **St. Moritz Lake Promenade:** Take a leisurely stroll along the Lake St. Moritz promenade for free. Enjoy views of the lake and the surrounding mountains.
- **Skiing on Corvatsch:** Experience skiing on Corvatsch. Prices for lift passes and equipment rentals vary.
- **Segantini Museum Visit:** Explore the Segantini Museum for around 18 CHF. Discover artworks by the renowned Italian painter Giovanni Segantini.
- **Cresta Run Spectating:** Watch the Cresta Run, a traditional toboggan track, for free. Marvel at the daring participants speeding down the course.
- **Engadin Museum Visit:** Visit the Engadine Museum for around 10 CHF. Learn about the cultural history of the Engadin region.
- **Bernina Express Day Trip:** Take a day trip on the Bernina Express to Tirano for approximately 70 CHF. Enjoy one of the most scenic train rides in the world.
- **Suvretta Loop Snowshoe Trail:** Explore the Suvretta Loop snowshoe trail for free. Enjoy a peaceful walk through snow-covered forests.
- **Night Sledding on Preda-Bergün:** Experience night sledding on the Preda-Bergün track for around 18 CHF. Glide down the illuminated course.
- **Corviglia Ice Cricket Match:** Attend the annual Corviglia Ice Cricket Match for free. Watch a unique cricket game played on the frozen lake.
- **Engadin St. Moritz Horse Racing on Ice:** Attend the horse racing on ice event for approximately 20 CHF. Witness horses galloping on the frozen lake.
- **St. Moritz Olympic Bob Run Tour:** Take a tour of the St. Moritz Olympic Bob Run for around 60 CHF. Learn about the history of bobsleigh.
- **Leaning Tower of St. Moritz:** Visit the Leaning Tower of St. Moritz for free. Discover the history behind this architectural curiosity.
- **Alpine Cheese Tasting:** Experience Alpine cheese tasting at a local dairy. Prices vary based on the selection of cheeses.

4. Cultural Events:

Free Concerts at Badrutt's Palace Hotel: Check for free concerts and cultural events hosted by Badrutt's Palace Hotel, which occasionally offers public performances in its grand setting.
Local Festivals in Nearby Villages: Explore nearby villages for local festivals and events that may feature free concerts, traditional performances, and cultural displays.
5. Budget-Friendly Transport:

Walking Trails: St. Moritz offers beautiful walking trails. Explore the surroundings on foot to appreciate the stunning landscapes, and consider hiking to nearby points of interest. By incorporating these budget-friendly tips, you can savor the elegance of St. Moritz, enjoy the Alpine beauty, and experience the Engadine culture without straining your budget, making your visit both economical and memorable.

Aspect	Money saving tips
Accommodation	Consider budget-friendly hotels like Hotel Laudinella, hostels such as St. Moritz Youth Hostel, or explore affordable options on booking platforms.
Transportation	Use the Engadin Mobil Card for free local transportation, explore the town on foot, and consider the Swiss Travel Pass for discounted regional travel.
Dining	Enjoy budget-friendly options at places like Chesa Veglia for Swiss specialties, cafes such as Hanselmann, and affordable eateries like Pavarotti & Friends.
Sightseeing	Stroll around Lake St. Moritz and explore the town on foot, take advantage of the Engadin Mobil Card for discounts on cable cars and local attractions.
Entertainment	Enjoy the natural beauty of the Engadin region, participate in free outdoor activities such as hiking or winter sports (depending on the season), and explore the local culture in St. Moritz.
Shopping	Explore budget-friendly shopping at Via Serlas and local markets for souvenirs and unique finds.
Day Trips	Plan a cost-effective day trip to Pontresina or Maloja using the efficient Swiss public transportation system.
Currency Exchange	Withdraw local currency from ATMs for better rates, avoid high fees by using local banks.
Timing	Visit during the shoulder seasons (spring or fall) for pleasant weather and potentially lower prices. Winter is also a great time for budget travelers, as it's the off-season for some luxury activities.
Technology	Use budget-friendly apps like Engadin St. Moritz for information, Maps.me for navigation, and local deal apps for discounts.

Jungfrau region

This breathtaking mountainous area renowned for its majestic peaks, charming villages, and unparalleled natural beauty. Home to iconic mountains like the Eiger, Mönch, and Jungfrau, this region offers a playground for outdoor enthusiasts and a haven for those seeking the grandeur of the Swiss Alps.

1. Affordable Accommodation:

Budget-Friendly Guesthouses: Consider staying in guesthouses in villages like Lauterbrunnen or Wengen. Options like Hotel Staubbach or Hotel Edelweiss offer affordable stays with mountain views.
Hostels in Interlaken: Explore hostels in Interlaken for budget-friendly accommodation. Take advantage of Interlaken's central location to access the Jungfrau region.

2. Cheap Eats:

Self-Catering Picnics: Purchase groceries in larger towns like Interlaken and pack a picnic for your excursions. Enjoy your meal with a backdrop of the stunning Jungfrau, Eiger, and Mönch mountains.
Mountain Hut Lunches: While mountain hut meals can be expensive, consider having lunch at lower-altitude huts for more budget-friendly options with equally stunning views.

3. Luxury for less

- **Jungfraujoch Top of Europe:** Take a day trip to Jungfraujoch for approximately 120 CHF. Experience panoramic views from the Sphinx Observatory and visit the Ice Palace.
- **Schilthorn Piz Gloria Cable Car:** Ride the cable car to Schilthorn Piz Gloria for around 70 CHF. Enjoy stunning views of the Eiger, Mönch, and Jungfrau peaks.
- **First Flyer Zipline in Grindelwald:** Experience the First Flyer Zipline in Grindelwald for approximately 40 CHF. Soar through the alpine landscapes for an exhilarating adventure.
- **Wengen-Männlichen Cable Car:** Take the cable car to Männlichen from Wengen for around 30 CHF. Enjoy panoramic views of the surrounding mountains.
- **Lauterbrunnen Valley Waterfalls Walk:** Take a walk through Lauterbrunnen Valley to see the iconic waterfalls. The walk is free, and you can explore at your own pace.
- **Grindelwald-First Mountain Cart Ride:** Experience the mountain cart ride on Grindelwald-First for around 34 CHF. Enjoy a thrilling descent with scenic views.
- **Mürren-Schilthorn Hiking Trail:** Hike from Mürren to Schilthorn for free. Immerse yourself in the stunning alpine scenery along this trail.
- **Trümmelbach Falls Visit:** Explore Trümmelbach Falls for around 12 CHF. Witness the power of glacial meltwater inside the mountain.
- **Kleine Scheidegg Mountain Railway Ride:** Take the mountain railway to Kleine Scheidegg for approximately 40 CHF. Enjoy views of the Eiger, Mönch, and Jungfrau.

- **Wengen Village Stroll:** Take a leisurely stroll through the car-free village of Wengen for free. Enjoy the charm of traditional Swiss architecture.
- **Mürren Via Ferrata:** Experience the Mürren Via Ferrata for around 100 CHF. Enjoy climbing with breathtaking views of the Lauterbrunnen Valley.
- **Grindelwald-Hike to Bachalpsee:** Hike to Bachalpsee from Grindelwald for free. Capture stunning reflections of the mountains in the alpine lake.
- **Lauterbrunnen Valley Bike Ride:** Rent a bike and explore Lauterbrunnen Valley. Bike rental prices vary, and you can enjoy the scenic ride at your own pace.
- **Männlichen Royal Walk:** Take the Royal Walk at Männlichen for approximately 20 CHF. Enjoy panoramic views and interactive installations.
- **Jungfrau Region Cheese Dairy Visit:** Visit a cheese dairy in the Jungfrau region for around 10 CHF. Learn about the traditional Swiss cheese-making process.
- **Gimmelwald Village Exploration:** Explore the charming village of Gimmelwald for free. Experience the tranquility of this alpine retreat.
- **Jungfrau Region Paragliding:** Experience paragliding in the Jungfrau region for around 150 CHF. Soar above the majestic peaks for a thrilling adventure.
- **Obersteinberg Mountain Hut Hike:** Hike to the Obersteinberg mountain hut for free. Enjoy a rustic mountain experience in a stunning setting.
- **Grindelwald First Mountain Restaurant Dining:** Indulge in dining at a mountain restaurant on Grindelwald First. While it may not be budget-friendly, the alpine ambiance is luxurious.
- **Jungfrau Region Spa Experience:** Treat yourself to a spa experience in the Jungfrau region. Prices vary depending on the chosen spa and treatment

4. Cultural Events:

Local Festivals: Check for local festivals and events happening in villages like Lauterbrunnen or Grindelwald. These events often showcase traditional music, dances, and cultural activities.
Alpine Museum in Jungfraujoch: While Jungfraujoch has a ticketed entry, visit the Alpine Sensation museum for free. It offers insights into the construction of the Jungfrau Railway.

5. Budget-Friendly Transport:

Regional Travel Passes: Invest in regional travel passes like the Jungfrau Travel Pass or the Bernese Oberland Regional Pass. These passes provide unlimited travel on trains, buses, and boats in the region.
Hiking Trails: Explore the many hiking trails in the Jungfrau region. Hiking is a budget-friendly way to experience the breathtaking landscapes and explore charming villages.
By combining these budget-friendly tips, you can immerse yourself in the natural beauty of the Jungfrau region, explore its picturesque villages, and gaze upon iconic mountain peaks without breaking the bank, making your visit both affordable and unforgettable.

Aspect	Money saving tips
Accommodation	Consider budget-friendly options like hostels such as Backpackers Villa Sonnenhof in Interlaken or Mountain Hostel in Lauterbrunnen, or explore affordable options on booking platforms.
Transportation	Use the local transportation passes like the Jungfrau Travel Pass or Regional Pass Bernese Oberland for discounted travel, explore towns on foot, and use public transportation for cost-effective travel between towns.
Dining	Enjoy budget-friendly options at local restaurants like Bäckerei-Konditorei Dind, cafes such as Restaurant Aelpli Wengen, and affordable eateries like Staubbachfall Restaurant in Lauterbrunnen.
Sightseeing	Explore the towns and landscapes on foot, take advantage of hiking trails, and use the Jungfrau Travel Pass for discounts on cable cars and attractions like Jungfraujoch.
Entertainment	Participate in free outdoor activities like hiking or enjoy the scenic beauty of the Jungfrau Region. Attend local events and festivals for cultural experiences.
Shopping	Explore budget-friendly shopping at local markets, souvenir shops in towns like Wengen, and Coop supermarkets for essentials.
Day Trips	Plan cost-effective day trips to nearby towns or attractions using the Jungfrau Travel Pass or Regional Pass Bernese Oberland.
Currency Exchange	Withdraw local currency from ATMs for better rates, avoid high fees by using local banks.
Timing	Visit during the shoulder seasons (spring or fall) for pleasant weather and potentially lower prices. Winter is also a great time for budget travelers, as it's the off-season for some activities.
Technology	Use budget-friendly apps like Jungfrau Region Travel Guide for information, Maps.me for navigation, and local deal apps for discounts.

Locarno

Locarno is a charming town that combines Mediterranean flair with Swiss efficiency. With its lakeside setting, historic architecture, and a lively cultural scene, Locarno invites visitors to experience a unique blend of relaxation and vibrancy in the heart of the Swiss-Italian landscape.

1. Affordable Accommodation:

Budget-Friendly Hotels: Consider staying in hotels like Hotel Belvedere Locarno or Hotel Garni Nessi for affordable yet comfortable accommodations in Locarno.
Hostels and Guesthouses: Explore hostels or guesthouses in the area, offering budget-friendly options with local character.

2. Cheap Eats:

Lakeside Picnic: Purchase fresh produce, cheese, and bread from local markets or grocery stores. Enjoy a budget-friendly lakeside picnic along the shores of Lake Maggiore.
Street Food at Piazza Grande: Visit Piazza Grande for street food vendors offering a variety of affordable and delicious options, especially during events and festivals.

3. Luxury for less

- **Cardada-Cimetta Cable Car:** Take the cable car to Cardada-Cimetta for approximately 25 CHF. Enjoy panoramic views of Lake Maggiore and the surrounding mountains.
- **Lido Locarno Beach:** Relax at Lido Locarno Beach for around 10 CHF. Enjoy the lakeside ambiance, swimming pools, and a sandy beach.
- **Parco delle Camelie (Camellia Park) Visit:** Explore Parco delle Camelie for around 5 CHF. Wander through the park featuring a stunning collection of camellias.
- **Falconry Locarno:** Attend a falconry show in Locarno for approximately 20 CHF. Experience the art of falconry with breathtaking bird displays.
- **Ascona Old Town Stroll:** Take a leisurely stroll through the charming old town of Ascona for free. Discover narrow streets, historic buildings, and lakeside promenades.
- **Casa Rusca Art Gallery:** Explore Casa Rusca Art Gallery for around 10 CHF. Admire a collection of Swiss and Italian art in a historic setting.
- **Isole di Brissago Boat Trip:** Take a boat trip to the Isole di Brissago for approximately 30 CHF. Explore the botanical gardens on the Brissago Islands.
- **Valle Verzasca Day Trip:** Take a day trip to Valle Verzasca for free. Enjoy the picturesque valley, visit the Roman bridge, and swim in crystal-clear river waters.
- **Monte Verità (Mountain of Truth) Hike:** Hike to Monte Verità for free. Enjoy scenic views and explore this historic hill known for its cultural significance.
- **Locarno Film Festival (During the Festival):** Attend the Locarno Film Festival for a unique cinematic experience. Ticket prices vary based on screenings and events.

- **Orselina Madonna del Sasso Visit:** Visit the sanctuary of Madonna del Sasso in Orselina for free. Enjoy panoramic views of Locarno and Lake Maggiore.
- **Tenero Outdoor Swimming Pool:** Relax at the Tenero outdoor swimming pool for around 8 CHF. Enjoy pools, slides, and a spacious sunbathing area.
- **Verzasca Dam Bungee Jump:** Experience bungee jumping from the Verzasca Dam for around 255 CHF. Enjoy an adrenaline-pumping adventure with scenic views.
- **Cardada Adventure Park:** Explore the Cardada Adventure Park for around 40 CHF. Enjoy tree-to-tree adventures and zip-lining.
- **Locarno Market Shopping:** Explore the Locarno market for free. Discover local products, crafts, and the lively atmosphere of the market.
- **Swissminiatur Visit:** Explore Swissminiatur for around 25 CHF. Experience a miniature Switzerland with replicas of famous landmarks.
- **Riding in the Centovalli:** Enjoy horseback riding in the Centovalli for approximately 80 CHF. Explore scenic trails in this picturesque region.
- **Intramonti Wine Tasting:** Experience wine tasting at Intramonti for approximately 20 CHF. Sample local wines in a beautiful vineyard setting.
- **Locarno Casino Visit:** Visit the Locarno Casino for free. While gaming may incur costs, explore the elegant casino and its surroundings.
- **Locarno Lakeside Promenade:** Take a lakeside stroll along the Locarno promenade for free. Enjoy views of Lake Maggiore and the surrounding mountains.

4. Cultural Events:

Free Concerts at Moon and Stars Festival: If visiting during the Moon and Stars Festival, check for free concerts or events that may take place in public spaces.
Open-Air Cinema in Piazza Grande: During the summer months, attend free screenings at the open-air cinema in Piazza Grande. It's a cultural experience under the stars.

5. Budget-Friendly Transport:

Locarno Card: Some accommodations offer a Locarno Card, providing free or discounted access to local transportation. Use buses or boats to explore the surrounding areas without additional expenses.
Walking and Biking: Locarno is a walkable city with scenic promenades. Consider renting a bike to explore the city and its surroundings in an affordable and eco-friendly way.
By incorporating these budget-friendly tips, you can experience the charm of Locarno, enjoy the lakeside atmosphere, and explore the cultural offerings without exceeding your budget, making your visit both economical and delightful.

Aspect	Money saving tips
Accommodation	Consider budget-friendly hotels like Hotel Garni Giacometti, hostels such as Youthhostel Locarno, or explore affordable options on booking platforms.
Transportation	Use the Ticino Ticket for free local transportation, explore the town on foot, and consider using boats on Lake Maggiore for a scenic and budget-friendly experience.
Dining	Enjoy budget-friendly options at local restaurants like Ristorante-Café Locarno, cafes such as Gelateria al Porto, and affordable eateries like Osteria Nostrana.
Sightseeing	Stroll along the lakeside promenade, explore the Piazza Grande and the Old Town (Città Vecchia) on foot, and take advantage of the Ticino Ticket for discounts on local attractions.
Entertainment	Relax by Lake Maggiore, attend free events in the Piazza Grande, and explore the nearby valleys for hiking or outdoor activities.
Shopping	Explore budget-friendly shopping at Via della Pace and local markets for souvenirs and unique finds.
Day Trips	Plan a cost-effective day trip to Ascona or the nearby Maggia Valley using public transportation.
Currency Exchange	Withdraw local currency from ATMs for better rates, avoid high fees by using local banks.
Timing	Visit during the shoulder seasons (spring or fall) for pleasant weather and potentially lower prices.
Technology	Use budget-friendly apps like Locarno Tourist Guide for information, Maps.me for navigation, and local deal apps for discounts.

Arosa

Arosa is a picturesque mountain resort town that captivates visitors with its stunning natural surroundings, outdoor recreational opportunities, and a welcoming alpine atmosphere. Known for its charm in both summer and winter, Arosa is a haven for those seeking tranquility, adventure, and the beauty of the Swiss mountains.

1. Affordable Accommodation:

Budget-Friendly Hotels and Guesthouses: Consider staying in hotels like Hotel Astoria or guesthouses in Arosa for budget-friendly yet comfortable accommodations.
Hostels in Chur: Explore hostels in nearby Chur for more budget-friendly options. A short train or bus ride connects Chur to Arosa, allowing you to enjoy both affordability and convenience.

2. Cheap Eats:

Local Bakeries and Cafes: Visit local bakeries and cafes for reasonably priced snacks and pastries. Enjoy Swiss specialties without breaking the bank.
Self-Catering Picnics: Purchase groceries from local stores and create your picnic. Arosa's natural landscapes provide a picturesque backdrop for a budget-friendly outdoor meal.

3. Luxury for less

- **Arosa-Lenzerheide Skiing:** Experience skiing in Arosa-Lenzerheide. Prices for lift passes and equipment rentals vary, providing options for different budgets.
- **Weisshorn Cable Car Ride:** Take the Weisshorn Cable Car for approximately 35 CHF. Enjoy panoramic views of the surrounding mountains.
- **Tschuggen Express Ski Lift:** Ski or snowboard using the Tschuggen Express Ski Lift for around 25 CHF. Access the slopes conveniently with this lift.
- **Arosa Bear Sanctuary Visit:** Explore the Arosa Bear Sanctuary for around 10 CHF. Witness rescued bears in a natural and spacious environment.
- **Obersee Lake Snowshoeing:** Enjoy snowshoeing around Obersee Lake for free. Experience the serenity of the snow-covered landscape.
- **Arosa-Weisshorn Hiking Trail:** Hike from Arosa to the Weisshorn for free. Marvel at the alpine scenery along this picturesque trail.
- **Arosa Rope Park:** Explore the Arosa Rope Park for approximately 50 CHF. Enjoy high ropes courses and zip-lining in a beautiful forest setting.
- **Obersee Lake Ice Skating:** Experience ice skating on Obersee Lake for around 10 CHF. Glide over the frozen lake with stunning mountain views.
- **Arosa Bärenland Trail:** Hike the Arosa Bärenland Trail for free. Enjoy a scenic trail with information about the local flora and fauna.
- **Täli Adventure Playground:** Visit the Täli Adventure Playground for free. Perfect for families, this playground offers fun in a mountainous setting.

- **Sattel-Hochstuckli Aerial Cableway Day Trip:** Take a day trip to Sattel-Hochstuckli Aerial Cableway for around 70 CHF. Experience the revolving gondola and panoramic views.
- **Arosa Parpaner Rothorn Railway Ride:** Take the Parpaner Rothorn Railway for approximately 25 CHF. Enjoy a nostalgic train ride with mountain views.
- **Arosa-Älplisee Hiking Trail:** Hike to Älplisee from Arosa for free. Experience the tranquility of this mountain lake.
- **Arosa Golf Course:** Enjoy a round of golf at the Arosa Golf Course. While it may not be budget-friendly, the course offers stunning alpine views.
- **Brüggerhorn Panorama Trail:** Hike the Brüggerhorn Panorama Trail for free. Experience breathtaking panoramic views of the surrounding mountains.
- **Bear Cave Visit:** Visit the Bear Cave in Arosa for around 5 CHF. Explore a cave with bear sculptures and learn about the local wildlife.
- **Arosa Music and Culture Events:** Attend music and cultural events in Arosa. Ticket prices vary based on performances and venues.
- **Hörnli Trail Running:** Experience trail running on the Hörnli Trail for free. Enjoy a challenging run with stunning mountain views.
- **Arosa Klangweg (Sound Trail):** Explore the Arosa Klangweg for free. Walk along this trail and experience nature through sound installations.
- **Arosa Spa and Wellness:** Treat yourself to spa and wellness services in Arosa. Prices vary based on treatments and facilities.

4. Cultural Events:

Local Festivals in Arosa: Check for local festivals and events happening in Arosa. These events often feature traditional music, dances, and cultural activities.
Open-Air Concerts: During the summer months, look out for open-air concerts or performances in public spaces. Arosa occasionally hosts free cultural events.

5. Budget-Friendly Transport:

Arosa Card: Some accommodations provide guests with an Arosa Card, offering free or discounted access to local transportation. Use buses or cable cars to explore the surrounding areas without additional expenses.
Walking and Skiing: Arosa is known for its walking and skiing trails. Enjoy the picturesque landscapes on foot during the warmer months or try cross-country skiing in winter.
By incorporating these budget-friendly tips, you can enjoy the alpine beauty of Arosa, experience local culture, and explore the outdoor offerings without overspending, making your visit both affordable and memorable.

Truly weird and wonderful things to do in Switzerland

Switzerland offers some unique and offbeat experiences that add a touch of whimsy and wonder to your visit. Here are a few truly weird and wonderful things to do:

- Igloo Village in Zermatt: Immerse yourself in the enchanting world of ice and snow by staying in an igloo at the Igloo Village in Zermatt. Prices vary based on the type of accommodation, ranging from 200 CHF to 500 CHF per person per night. Experience the magic of spending a night in a cozy igloo under the starry Swiss sky.
- HR Giger Museum, Gruyères: Delve into the surreal and otherworldly at the HR Giger Museum in Gruyères. The admission price, around 12 CHF for adults and 4 CHF for children, grants access to the captivating works of the renowned Swiss artist H.R. Giger, famous for his design work on the film "Alien."
- The Charlie Chaplin Museum, Vevey: Step into the world of silent film legend Charlie Chaplin at the Charlie Chaplin Museum in Vevey. For approximately 25 CHF for adults, 15 CHF for seniors and students, and free admission for children under 6, explore the life and artistry of one of cinema's greatest icons.
- Trümmelbach Falls Inside a Mountain: Witness the extraordinary power of nature at Trümmelbach Falls in the heart of the Lauterbrunnen Valley. For around 12 CHF for adults and 4 CHF for children, venture inside the mountain to experience the thundering waterfalls cascading through a series of tunnels.
- Kindli Burning, Liestal: Attend the "Chienbäse" festival in Liestal, where flaming bundles of pinewood are paraded through the streets. While attending the festival is typically free, there may be costs associated with participating in certain activities or events during this fiery and vibrant celebration.
- Swiss Vapeur Parc, Le Bouveret: Embark on a miniature adventure at Swiss Vapeur Parc, where a world of model trains awaits. The admission price, around 24 CHF for adults, 12 CHF for children aged 4-15, and free for children under 4, grants access to this charming miniature railway park.
- Felsenegg Cliff Walk, Lake Zurich: Take a thrilling walk along the Felsenegg Cliff Walk overlooking Lake Zurich. The cost of taking the Felsenegg cable car is approximately 30 CHF for adults and 10 CHF for children, with access to the Cliff Walk possibly included in the cable car ticket.
- Yodeling Festival: Immerse yourself in the tradition of yodeling at one of Switzerland's traditional yodeling festivals. Admission prices vary, ranging from 20 CHF to 50 CHF, offering you a unique opportunity to experience the soulful and captivating art of yodeling in the Swiss Alps.

Best Adrenaline Thrills

Switzerland offers a range of adrenaline-pumping activities amid its stunning landscapes. Here are some thrilling experiences with approximate prices:

- **Paragliding in Interlaken:**
    - **Price:** Around CHF 150 to CHF 200.
    - **Details:** Soar above the Interlaken region, enjoying breathtaking views of the Swiss Alps while tandem paragliding.
- **Skydiving in Lauterbrunnen:**
    - **Price:** Approximately CHF 400 to CHF 450.
    - **Details:** Experience the ultimate thrill of freefalling with a tandem skydiving jump near the iconic Lauterbrunnen Valley.
- **Canyoning in Ticino:**
    - **Price:** Typically CHF 100 to CHF 150.
    - **Details:** Navigate through narrow gorges, jump off cliffs, and rappel down waterfalls for an exhilarating canyoning adventure in the Swiss Italian region of Ticino.
- **Bungee Jumping at Contra Dam:**
    - **Price:** Around CHF 200 to CHF 250.
    - **Details:** Take a leap off the Contra Dam, famously featured in a James Bond movie, for a thrilling bungee jumping experience.
- **White Water Rafting in the Alps:**
    - **Price:** Prices vary, but expect to pay around CHF 80 to CHF 120.
    - **Details:** Navigate the rapids of Swiss rivers, such as the Lütschine or the Inn River, for an adrenaline-charged white water rafting adventure.
- **Via Ferrata in the Engadin:**
    - **Price:** Typically CHF 80 to CHF 120 for guided tours.
    - **Details:** Scale vertical rock faces and traverse exposed ledges in the Engadin region with guided via ferrata experiences.
- **Mountain Carting in Grindelwald:**
    - **Price:** Approximately CHF 50 to CHF 70.
    - **Details:** Race down mountain trails on specially designed carts for an exciting mountain carting experience in Grindelwald.

Take a cooking class

Switzerland offers various cooking classes that provide hands-on experiences with Swiss cuisine. While specific prices can vary, and it's advisable to check the latest rates on the respective websites, here are some cooking classes you might consider:

Vevey, Lavaux: L'Atelier de Grand-Maman
This culinary workshop in Vevey offers classes in a traditional Swiss kitchen setting. Prices can vary based on the specific class, but they often start around CHF 90-150 per person.

Zurich: Culinary Arts Academy
The Culinary Arts Academy in Zurich occasionally offers cooking classes to the public. Prices can range from CHF 100-200, depending on the class and duration.

Lucerne: Swiss Cooking Academy
The Swiss Cooking Academy in Lucerne provides classes on Swiss cuisine. Prices can start from CHF 100 and go up, depending on the type of class and ingredients used.

Go Swimming

While you may not stay somewhere with a pool, you can visit Switzerland's public swimming pools, both indoor and outdoor, where you can enjoy a refreshing swim. Here are some notable public swimming pools in different regions of Switzerland, along with general information on prices:

Oberried Swimming Pool (Badi Oberried), Bern:
   Location: Bern
   Features: Outdoor pool with stunning views of the surrounding mountains.
   Prices: Admission prices may vary, but they typically range from CHF 5 to CHF 10 for adults.

Seebad Enge, Zurich:
   Location: Zurich
   Features: A lakeside swimming area with a large sunbathing lawn.
   Prices: Admission prices vary, but expect to pay around CHF 8 to CHF 10 for adults.

Thermalbad & Spa Zurich:
   Location: Zurich
   Features: Indoor thermal baths and spa facilities.
   Prices: Thermal bath entrance typically ranges from CHF 35 to CHF 40 for adults.

Migros Sport- und Erlebnisbad, Lausanne:
   Location: Lausanne
   Features: An indoor and outdoor pool complex with water slides and wellness facilities.
   Prices: Admission prices vary, but they typically range from CHF 10 to CHF 20 for adults.

Piscine de Bellerive, Geneva:
   Location: Geneva
   Features: Lakeside outdoor pool with a beach area.
   Prices: Admission prices vary, but they typically range from CHF 5 to CHF 10 for adults.

Freibad Marzili, Bern:
   Location: Bern
   Features: Outdoor pool located along the Aare River.
   Prices: Admission prices may vary, but they typically range from CHF 5 to CHF 10 for adults.

Aquabasilea, Pratteln:
   Location: Pratteln (near Basel)
   Features: One of the largest water parks in Switzerland with various pools and slides.
   Prices: Admission prices vary, but they typically range from CHF 30 to CHF 40 for adults.

Schwimmbad St. Jakob, Basel:
   Location: Basel
   Features: Outdoor and indoor pools with various amenities.

Prices: Admission prices may vary, but they typically range from CHF 8 to CHF 15 for adults.

Sports in Switzerland

Switzerland offers a variety of sports, and attending a live game can be an exciting experience. Here are some popular sports and ways to catch a game more affordably:

Football (Soccer):
Popular Teams: FC Basel, BSC Young Boys, FC Zurich, and FC Lausanne-Sport are among the notable football clubs.
Affordable Tickets: Look for discounted tickets, especially for matches against lower-ranked teams. Consider attending cup matches or midweek fixtures for potentially lower prices.

Ice Hockey:
Popular Teams: HC Davos, SC Bern, and ZSC Lions are well-known ice hockey teams.
Affordable Tickets: Check for weekday games or matches against less popular opponents. Some teams offer discounted family packages.

Basketball:
Swiss Basketball League: Attend games in the Swiss Basketball League featuring teams like Fribourg Olympic and Lions de Genève.
Affordable Tickets: Look for promotional nights or special discounts for students and youth.

Tennis:
Swiss Indoors (Tennis): Basel hosts the Swiss Indoors, an ATP 500 event attracting top tennis players.
Affordable Tickets: Consider attending early-round matches or qualifying rounds for lower-priced tickets.

Handball:
Swiss Handball League: Teams like Pfadi Winterthur and Kadetten Schaffhausen compete in the Swiss Handball League.
Affordable Tickets: Check for group discounts or promotions during specific matchdays.

Volleyball:
Swiss Volleyball League: Teams like Lausanne Morges UC and Volley Amriswil compete in the Swiss Volleyball League.
Affordable Tickets: Look for student discounts or special promotions for home games.

Rugby:
Swiss Rugby Super League: Teams like Hermance RRC and CERN Meyrin Rugby Club participate in the Swiss Rugby Super League.
Affordable Tickets: Rugby matches often have a more casual atmosphere, and tickets may be reasonably priced.

To catch a game more cheaply:

Check Official Websites: Visit the official websites of sports teams or leagues for information on ticket prices and promotions.

Hidden spots

Switzerland is filled with hidden gems that offer unique experiences, often away from the well-trodden tourist paths. Here are 20 hidden spots in Switzerland along with budget-friendly activities you can enjoy:

Caumasee, Flims:
Activity: Relax by the turquoise waters of Caumasee and take a swim in the lake.
Budget Tip: Bring a picnic, and enjoy the beautiful surroundings without spending much.

Ruinaulta Gorge, Graubünden:
Activity: Hike or bike through the stunning Rhine Gorge, known as the "Swiss Grand Canyon."
Budget Tip: Pack your own snacks and explore the trails on foot or by bike.

Creux du Van, Neuchâtel:
Activity: Hike to the natural amphitheater, Creux du Van, for breathtaking views.
Budget Tip: Hiking is free, so enjoy the landscapes without additional costs.

Lauterbrunnen Valley, Bernese Oberland:
Activity: Explore the picturesque Lauterbrunnen Valley with its numerous waterfalls.
Budget Tip: Take a nature walk and enjoy the waterfalls for free.

Schwarzsee, Fribourg:
Activity: Hike to Schwarzsee (Black Lake) and enjoy the scenic mountain views.
Budget Tip: Bring your own snacks, and appreciate the tranquility of the lake.

The Aare Gorge, Meiringen:
Activity: Walk through the narrow Aare Gorge and witness the impressive rock formations.
Budget Tip: Entrance fees are reasonable, and it's a unique natural spectacle.

Gruyères Village, Fribourg:
Activity: Explore the charming medieval village of Gruyères.
Budget Tip: Wander through the cobblestone streets, and consider buying local cheese for a picnic.

Oeschinensee, Bernese Oberland:
Activity: Take a hike to Oeschinensee, a stunning mountain lake.
Budget Tip: Hiking is free, and you can enjoy the scenery without spending much.

Emmental, Bern:
Activity: Visit the picturesque Emmental region known for its rolling hills and traditional Swiss farms.
Budget Tip: Take a self-guided walking tour and savor the rural landscapes.

Mürren, Bernese Oberland:
Activity: Explore the car-free village of Mürren and take in panoramic views.
Budget Tip: Enjoy a scenic hike and capture the beauty of the Swiss Alps.

Stein am Rhein, Schaffhausen:
  Activity: Wander through the well-preserved medieval town of Stein am Rhein.
  Budget Tip: Stroll through the charming streets and admire the historical architecture.

Lake Brienz, Bernese Oberland:
  Activity: Take a boat trip on Lake Brienz and enjoy the surrounding mountains.
  Budget Tip: Opt for a ferry ride, which can be more affordable than private boat rentals.

Valley of Verzasca, Ticino:
  Activity: Visit the stunning Verzasca Dam and the crystal-clear river.
  Budget Tip: Explore the valley on foot, and perhaps take a dip in the refreshing waters.

Muottas Muragl, Engadin:
  Activity: Take the funicular to Muottas Muragl for panoramic views of the Engadin valley.
  Budget Tip: Hike to the viewpoint instead of taking the funicular to save on costs.

Trummelbach Falls, Lauterbrunnen:
  Activity: Witness the impressive underground waterfalls inside the mountain.
  Budget Tip: Purchase a combined ticket for multiple attractions in the Lauterbrunnen Valley.

Rapperswil, Zurich:
  Activity: Explore the "town of roses" on the shores of Lake Zurich.
  Budget Tip: Walk around the charming old town and enjoy the lakeside promenade.

Aletsch Glacier, Valais:
  Activity: Hike near the Aletsch Glacier, the largest glacier in the Alps.
  Budget Tip: Guided glacier hikes can be more affordable in groups.

Bregaglia Valley, Graubünden:
  Activity: Discover the scenic Bregaglia Valley with its traditional Engadin architecture.
  Budget Tip: Enjoy a self-guided walking tour through the valley.

Rhine Falls, Schaffhausen:
  Activity: Witness the largest waterfall in Europe, Rhine Falls.
  Budget Tip: Explore the viewing platforms and take in the spectacle for free.

Brissago Islands, Ticino:
  Activity: Visit the botanical gardens on the Brissago Islands in Lake Maggiore.
  Budget Tip: Combine a boat trip with a visit to the gardens for a reasonable day out.

Best place to find Bargains

In Switzerland, finding bargains often involves exploring thrift stores, second-hand shops, and flea markets. Here are some places where you can hunt for bargains:

Brockenhaus (Thrift Stores):
Description: Brockenhaus refers to thrift stores in Switzerland. These stores often sell second-hand clothing, furniture, and various household items.
Location: Major cities and towns have Brockenhaus stores. Zurich, Geneva, and Bern are good places to start.

Kilo Shops (Thrift by the Kilo):
Description: Some thrift shops in Switzerland operate on a "thrift by the kilo" system. You pay based on the weight of the items you choose.
Location: Cities like Zurich and Basel may have kilo shops. Check local directories or online platforms for specific locations.

Flea Markets (Brocantes/Flohmarkt):
Description: Flea markets are popular for finding second-hand treasures, antiques, and unique items. Vendors often sell a variety of goods.
Location: Major cities and towns host flea markets regularly. Zurich's Helvetiaplatz Flea Market and Geneva's Plainpalais Flea Market are well-known.

Ricardo.ch:
Description: Ricardo is an online marketplace where individuals sell new and used items. You can find a variety of products, including clothing, electronics, and furniture.
Website: Ricardo.ch

Tutti.ch:
Description: Tutti is another online marketplace similar to Ricardo, where people sell and buy second-hand items.
Website: Tutti.ch

Caritas Shops:
Description: Caritas is a charitable organization with thrift shops across Switzerland. They offer affordable second-hand goods, and the proceeds support social projects.
Location: Look for Caritas shops in various cities and towns.

Emmaus Switzerland:
Description: Emmaus is an international solidarity movement with branches in Switzerland. They operate thrift stores and sell second-hand items.
Location: Find Emmaus shops in cities like Geneva and Lausanne.

What to do in Switzerland for free at night

Switzerland offers various free activities to enjoy at night, allowing you to experience the country's beauty and culture after sunset without spending money. Here are some suggestions:

Night Strolls in Old Towns:
Explore the charming old towns of cities like Zurich, Geneva, or Bern. Wander through narrow cobblestone streets, admire historical architecture, and experience the unique atmosphere of these places.

Lake Geneva Promenade:
Enjoy a leisurely stroll along the promenade of Lake Geneva. Take in the sparkling lights, enjoy the lake breeze, and appreciate the views of the city.

Rhine River in Basel:
Walk along the Rhine River in Basel. The illuminated bridges and buildings create a picturesque setting. You can also watch locals swimming in the Rhine during the warmer months.

Stargazing in the Swiss Alps:
Head to a dark spot in the Swiss Alps away from city lights. On clear nights, stargazing can be a mesmerizing experience. Identify constellations and enjoy the peaceful mountain environment.

Public Art Installations:
Many Swiss cities feature public art installations that are often illuminated at night. Check out sculptures, light displays, or interactive art pieces in public spaces.

Lakeside Reflections in Lucerne:
Visit the shores of Lake Lucerne at night. The reflections of the lights on the water, combined with the mountains in the background, create a magical atmosphere.

Street Performances and Buskers:
Keep an eye out for street performers and buskers in city centers. Street art and live performances add vibrancy to the nightlife in places like Zurich's Niederdorf area.

Night Markets and Festivals:
Attend free night markets or cultural festivals that occasionally take place in various Swiss cities. These events often feature live music, performances, and food stalls.

Lively Atmosphere in Lausanne's Flon District:
Visit the Flon district in Lausanne, known for its vibrant nightlife. While some venues may have cover charges, you can still enjoy the lively atmosphere and architecture.

Botanical Gardens:
Some botanical gardens, like the one in Geneva, remain open during the evening. Explore these tranquil settings and appreciate the beauty of the plants and landscapes.

University Campuses:
University campuses often have open spaces where you can relax, read, or simply enjoy the surroundings. Some campuses may host evening events or lectures that are open to the public.

How to get out of Switzerland cheaply

Cheapest Buses:
- **FlixBus:** FlixBus is a popular long-distance bus service operating in Europe, offering budget-friendly travel options to various destinations. It often provides competitive rates for routes both within Switzerland and to neighboring countries.

Cheapest Trains:
- **SBB (Swiss Federal Railways):** The national railway company, SBB, provides an extensive and efficient train network in Switzerland. While train travel in Switzerland is generally not considered cheap, SBB offers various promotions, discounts, and saver passes, especially if you book in advance.

Cheapest Flight Operators:
- **EasyJet:** EasyJet is a low-cost airline that operates flights within Europe, including Switzerland. It's known for offering competitive prices, particularly if you book well in advance and are flexible with your travel dates.
- **Ryanair:** Ryanair is another budget airline that serves various European destinations, providing affordable flight options. As with any budget airline, be aware of additional fees for services that may be included in the fares of other carriers.
- **Wizz Air:** Wizz Air is a low-cost airline that focuses on flights to and from Eastern and Central Europe. While it may not have an extensive presence in Switzerland, it could be an option for certain routes.

Airport lounges in Switzerland

Airport lounges are the best way to relax before a flight. Here are a few lounges in major Swiss airports along with estimated prices (please note that prices are subject to change):

Zurich Airport (ZRH):
    Aspire Lounge:
        Price: Starting from around 38 CHF (Swiss Francs) for access.
        Amenities: Wi-Fi, snacks, beverages, and comfortable seating.
    SWISS Business Lounge:
        Price: Included for SWISS Business Class passengers.
        Amenities: Business services, showers, and a selection of food and drinks.
    SkyTeam Lounge:
        Price: Starting from around 38 CHF for access.
        Amenities: Wi-Fi, international newspapers, and refreshments.

Geneva Airport (GVA):
    Dnata SkyView Lounge:
        Price: Starting from around 38 CHF for access.
        Amenities: Snacks, beverages, Wi-Fi, and comfortable seating.
    SWISS Business Lounge:
        Price: Included for SWISS Business Class passengers.

Amenities: Business services, showers, and a selection of food and drinks.

Basel-Mulhouse Airport (BSL/MLH):
- EuroAirport Skyview Lounge:
  - *Price:* Starting from around 35 EUR (Euros) for access.
  - *Amenities:* Wi-Fi, snacks, beverages, and a relaxing environment.
- SWISS Business Lounge:
  - *Price:* Included for SWISS Business Class passengers.
  - *Amenities:* Business services, showers, and a selection of food and drinks.

Languages

Switzerland is a multilingual country with four official languages. The linguistic diversity reflects the country's cultural richness and historical influences. The four official languages of Switzerland are:

German:
Spoken in the central and northern regions of Switzerland, including cities such as Zurich, Bern, and Basel.
French:
Spoken in the western part of Switzerland, in cities like Geneva, Lausanne, and Neuchâtel.
Italian:
Spoken in the southern part of Switzerland, primarily in the canton of Ticino and some areas of Graubünden.
Romansh:
Spoken in some parts of the canton of Graubünden, particularly in the southeastern mountainous regions. Romansh has several dialects.

These language divisions are often aligned with the different cantons of Switzerland. The linguistic diversity adds to the cultural richness of the country, and residents are typically proficient in multiple languages. In addition to the official languages, English is also widely spoken, especially in urban areas and within the younger population.

Swiss German with English pronunciation

Swiss German is a variant of the German language spoken in Switzerland, and it has several distinctive features that set it apart from other types of German, particularly the Standard German spoken in Germany.

Hello / Hi - Grüezi / Hoi (grew-et-see / hoy)
Goodbye - Adieu / Tschüss (ah-dyoo / chus)
Please - Bitte (bit-teh)
Thank you - Merci / Danke (mer-see / dahn-keh)
You're welcome - Bitte schön (bit-teh shern)
Excuse me / I'm sorry - Entschuldigung (ent-shool-dee-goong)
Yes - Ja (yah)
No - Nein (nine)
How are you? - Wie goht's? (vee gohts)
I'm fine, thank you - Mir goht's guet, merci (meer gohts gwet, mer-see)
What's your name? - Wie heißt du? (vee hyst doo)

My name is... - Ig heiss... (eek hys)
Where is the bathroom? - Wo isch d'Toilette? (vo ish d'twa-let-uh)
I don't understand - Ich versteh's nit (eek fer-shtays nit)
Can you help me? - Chasch mir hälfe? (kash meer help-eh)
I need... - Ich bruche... (eek broo-khuh)
Good morning - Guete Morge (gwet-eh mor-geh)
Good evening - Guete Abe (gwet-eh ah-beh)
Good night - Guet Nacht (gwet naakht)
Cheers! / Prost! - Proscht! (prohst)

Swiss French with English pronunciation:

Hello / Hi - Bonjour / Salut (bon-zhoor / sah-loo)
Goodbye - Au revoir (oh-rev-wah)
Please - S'il vous plaît (seel voo pleh)
Thank you - Merci (mer-see)
You're welcome - De rien (duh ree-ehn)
Excuse me / I'm sorry - Excusez-moi (ex-kew-zay mwah)
Yes - Oui (wee)
No - Non (noh)
How are you? - Comment ça va? (koh-mah sah vah)
I'm fine, thank you - Ça va bien, merci (sah vah byen, mer-see)
What's your name? - Comment tu t'appelles? (koh-mah too tah-pel)
My name is... - Je m'appelle... (zhuh mah-pel)
Where is the bathroom? - Où sont les toilettes? (oo sohn lay twa-let)
I don't understand - Je ne comprends pas (zhuh nuh kohm-prahnd pah)
Can you help me? - Pouvez-vous m'aider? (poo-veh voo may-dey)
I need... - J'ai besoin de... (zhay buh-zwah duh)
Good morning - Bonjour (bon-zhoor)
Good evening - Bonsoir (bon-swahr)
Good night - Bonne nuit (bun nwee)
Cheers! / Santé! - Santé (sahn-tay)

Swiss Italian with English pronunciation

Hello / Hi:
Swiss Italian: Ciao (chow)
Pronunciation: chow
Good morning:
Swiss Italian: Buongiorno (bwohn-jor-no)
Pronunciation: bwohn-jor-no
Good afternoon / Good evening:
Swiss Italian: Buonasera (bwoh-na-seh-ra)
Pronunciation: bwoh-na-seh-ra
Good night:
Swiss Italian: Buonanotte (bwoh-na-not-teh)
Pronunciation: bwoh-na-not-teh
How are you?:
Swiss Italian: Come stai? (koh-meh stai)
Pronunciation: koh-meh stai
Thank you:
Swiss Italian: Grazie (gra-tsye)
Pronunciation: gra-tsye
You're welcome:
Swiss Italian: Prego (pre-go)
Pronunciation: pre-go
Excuse me / I'm sorry:
Swiss Italian: Scusa / Mi dispiace (skoo-sa / mee dees-pya-che)
Pronunciation: skoo-sa / mee dees-pya-che
Please:
Swiss Italian: Per favore (per fa-vo-re)
Pronunciation: per fa-vo-re
Yes:
Swiss Italian: Sì (see)
Pronunciation: see
No:
Swiss Italian: No (no)
Pronunciation: no
Do you speak English?:
Swiss Italian: Parli inglese? (par-lee een-gle-se)
Pronunciation: par-lee een-gle-se
Where is the bathroom?:
Swiss Italian: Dov'è il bagno? (do-ve il ban-yo)
Pronunciation: do-ve il ban-yo
How much does this cost?:
Swiss Italian: Quanto costa questo? (kwan-to kosta kwe-sto)
Pronunciation: kwan-to kosta kwe-sto
I don't understand:
Swiss Italian: Non capisco (non ka-pee-sko)
Pronunciation: non ka-pee-sko

Scams

While Switzerland is generally considered safe for tourists, it's always wise to be aware of potential scams that can occur in any destination. Here are some tourist scams to be cautious of in Switzerland:

Fake Police Officers:
Be wary of individuals posing as police officers asking to see your passport or valuables. Legitimate police officers will have proper identification, and you can ask to see it.

Distraction Thefts:
Beware of distractions, such as someone spilling something on you or dropping items near you. While you're focused on the distraction, an accomplice may attempt to steal your belongings.

ATM Skimming:
Check ATMs for any suspicious devices or attachments before using them. Criminals may install skimming devices to capture your card information.

Unofficial Tour Guides:
Avoid accepting services from unofficial tour guides who approach you on the street. Stick to reputable tour operators and guides to ensure your safety and the quality of the experience.

Overpriced Taxis:
Use official taxi services and be sure that the meter is running. Avoid unmarked or unregistered vehicles that may overcharge tourists.

Fake Goods:
When shopping for souvenirs, be cautious of counterfeit goods. Stick to reputable shops and markets, and check the authenticity of products.

Restaurant Bill Padding:
Check your restaurant bill carefully for any additional or inflated charges. Some unscrupulous establishments may attempt to pad the bill with extra items.

Petty Theft in Crowded Places:
Be vigilant in crowded areas, such as public transportation or popular tourist attractions, as pickpocketing can occur. Keep your belongings secure and be aware of your surroundings.

Fake Charity Solicitations:
Exercise caution when approached by individuals claiming to represent charities. Verify their legitimacy before making any donations.

Rental Car Scams:
Inspect rental cars thoroughly before accepting them and document any pre-existing damage. Some rental companies may attempt to charge for damage that was already present.

"Gold Ring" Scam:
In tourist areas, you may encounter individuals claiming to have found a gold ring and offering it to you. They will then demand money in return. Avoid engaging in such transactions.

Common complaints of tourists visiting Switzerland with solutions

Complaint: High Cost of Food	Solution: Get most of your food from the too good to go app. It will save you at least $2,000 on food. Opt for local markets, grocery stores, and affordable restaurants. Picnics with fresh, local products can be a cost-effective and enjoyable dining option.
Complaint: Limited Transportation Options	Solution: Switzerland has an extensive and efficient public transportation system. Plan your itinerary to make the most of trains, buses, and boats, which is more economical than renting a car.
Complaint: Weather-Related Disruptions	Solution: Switzerland's weather can be unpredictable. Check weather forecasts and plan indoor activities for days with adverse conditions. Bring appropriate clothing for varying weather.
Complaint: Language Barriers	Solution: Learn a few basic phrases in the local language (German, French, Italian, or Romansh). English is widely understood, but making an effort to communicate in the local language is appreciated.
Complaint: Crowded Tourist Attractions	Solution: Visit popular attractions early in the morning or later in the day to avoid peak hours. Consider exploring off-the-beaten-path destinations for a more relaxed experience.
Complaint: Lack of Free Wi-Fi	Solution: Many hotels, cafes, and public spaces offer free Wi-Fi. Additionally, consider purchasing a local SIM card for data access during your stay.
Complaint: Limited Nightlife Options	Solution: While Switzerland may not have a reputation for vibrant nightlife, cities like Zurich and Geneva offer a range of bars and clubs. Check local events and explore the nightlife scene.
Complaint: Strict Store Hours	Solution: Plan shopping during regular store hours, and be aware that some smaller towns and rural areas may have more limited hours. Stock up on essentials in advance.
Complaint: Overcrowded Ski Resorts	Solution: Consider visiting lesser-known ski resorts or plan your trip during the shoulder seasons. Avoid peak holiday periods for a quieter experience on the slopes.
Complaint: Difficulty Finding Vegetarian/Vegan Options	Solution: Inquire about vegetarian or vegan options in restaurants, and explore health food stores and specialty restaurants that cater to dietary preferences.
Complaint: Lack of Cultural Understanding	Solution: Familiarize yourself with Swiss customs and cultural norms. Respect local traditions, such as quiet hours, and learn about the country's history and heritage.
Complaint: Tourist Traps	Solution: Research restaurants and attractions in advance, read reviews, and seek recommendations from locals to avoid falling into tourist traps.
Complaint: Complicated Train Schedules	Solution: Use online resources and apps to simplify train schedules. Swiss public transportation websites offer user-friendly tools to plan your journeys.
Complaint: Hiking Trails Are Too Difficult	Solution: Switzerland has hiking trails suitable for various skill levels. Research trails that match your fitness level and choose routes with manageable difficulty.
Complaint: Lack of Interactivity in Museums	Solution: Look for guided tours or interactive exhibits in museums. Some museums offer apps or audio guides to enhance the visitor experience.
Complaint: Difficulty Finding Public Restrooms	Solution: Use restrooms in train stations, shopping malls, and public buildings. Carry a small amount of change, as some public restrooms may have nominal fees.
Complaint: Strict Smoking Regulations	Solution: Abide by Switzerland's smoking regulations, which may restrict smoking in certain public areas. Be aware of designated smoking zones and respect local ordinances.

Embrace the Swiss Way of Life

As you embark on your Swiss adventure, you'll quickly discover that it's not just about breathtaking mountains and pristine lakes – it's a lifestyle that blends tradition, precision, and a touch of chocolate-induced joy.

The Art of Punctuality:

Switzerland takes time seriously, and that's not just because they produce the world's finest watches. When the clock strikes, everything runs with Swiss precision. Trains glide into stations on the dot, and meetings start with a punctuality that could put a Swiss watch to shame. So, synchronize your watch and embrace the timely rhythm of Swiss life.

Multilingual Magic:

With four official languages, Switzerland is a linguistic marvel. In the German-speaking regions, greet with a cheerful "Grüezi," while in the French areas, say "Bonjour" with a touch of finesse. In Italian-speaking cantons, "Buongiorno" sets the right tone, and in Romansh regions, well, you might pick up a few enchanting phrases.

The Culinary Symphony:

Swiss cuisine is a delightful symphony of flavors, and fondue is the star performer. Dive into a pot of melted cheese with friends or family, and you'll understand why the Swiss take this communal dining experience seriously. Don't forget to savor Swiss chocolate – it's practically a national treasure. Indulge your taste buds and thank the Swiss cows for their contribution to the delectable cheese and chocolate creations.

Alpine Etiquette:

Venturing into the Swiss Alps? Hiking and skiing aren't just activities; they're a way of life. Embrace the Alpine spirit by greeting fellow hikers with a friendly "Hoi" on the trails. If you're exploring in winter, take a moment to sip on some mulled wine at a cozy mountain hut – the Swiss way of warming up after a day in the snow.

Precision in Every Detail:

Swiss precision extends beyond watches. It's in the immaculate cleanliness of the cities, the efficiency of public transportation, and even in the meticulous presentation of Swiss chocolate. Enjoy the organized chaos of a Swiss train station – trains departing and arriving with mathematical precision, like a beautifully choreographed dance.

Alpine Tradition Meets Modernity:

Switzerland seamlessly blends tradition with modernity. Wander through charming medieval towns, where cobblestone streets lead to contemporary boutiques. The Swiss have mastered the art of preserving their heritage while embracing the innovations of the 21st century.

So, dear reader, as you soak in the stunning landscapes, relish the delectable cuisine, and embrace the clockwork precision, you're not just experiencing Switzerland – you're living the Swiss way of life. Take a deep breath of that crisp Alpine air and let the rhythm of this enchanting country capture your heart. Willkommen in der Schweiz – welcome to Switzerland!

Recap: How to have a $10,000 Trip to Switzerland for $1,000

Tips for Cost-Effective Travel in Switzerland	Potential Savings
Travel during Off-Peak Seasons	$3,000
Mountain huts and farm stay Accommodations. Mid week five-star hotel stays	$3,000
Swiss Travel Pass	$2,000
Free City Tours	$300
Too Good to go bags	$2,000
Water Fountains	$100
Hike Instead of Cable Cars	$200
Free Outdoor Activities	-
Museum Free Days	$200
Discount City Cards	$2,500
Bike Rentals	$100
Book accommodation, cable cars and trains in Advance	$1,500
Local Festivals	Free
Use currency converted Card (convert your money to CHF to avoid conversion fees)	$500
Potential Savings	**$11,300**

Luxury Trip to Switzerland on a Budget Checklist

**1. Travel Planning:
- Research and plan your trip during the shoulder seasons (spring or fall) for potential cost savings.
- Consider flying into less expensive airports or nearby cities.

2. Accommodation:
- Look for budget-friendly luxury hotels or boutique accommodations.
- Explore options like Airbnb or guesthouses for a more local experience.
- Check for deals and discounts on accommodation booking platforms.

3. Transportation:
- Utilize public transportation, such as trains and buses, which are efficient and well-connected.
- Consider purchasing a Swiss Travel Pass for unlimited travel on trains, buses, and boats if you will travel on consecutive days. Otherwise pre-book train or bus tickets for super saver deals.

4. Dining:
- Choose local markets and street food for some meals to save on dining expenses.
- Research affordable yet high-quality restaurants or cafes with local cuisine.
- Take advantage of too goof to go hotel breakfasts, lunches and dinners. You can eat like royalty for a fraction of the cost using this app.

5. Activities:
- Prioritize free or low-cost activities such as hiking, exploring charming towns, and enjoying nature.
- Check for city passes or attraction bundles to save on entrance fees.
- Look for discounted tickets for cultural events or museums.

6. Wellness and Spa:
- Explore local thermal baths or spas that offer day passes or discounts during off-peak hours.

7. Shopping:
- Shop at local markets for souvenirs and unique items.
- Look for outlet stores for luxury brands at discounted prices.

8. Currency Exchange:
- Exchange currency at local banks or use ATM withdrawals for better rates.
- Be mindful of transaction fees and choose financial services with lower costs.

9. Communication:
- Use local SIM cards or international roaming packages to save on communication costs.
- Take advantage of free Wi-Fi available in hotels and public spaces.

10. Flexibility:
- Stay flexible with your itinerary to take advantage of last-minute deals or promotions.
- Be open to exploring lesser-known destinations for unique experiences.

12. Travel Insurance:
- Ensure you have comprehensive travel insurance to cover unexpected expenses.

Remember: Prioritize experiences over material luxuries, and savor the breathtaking natural beauty that Switzerland has to offer

Money Mistakes to Avoid

Mistake	Solution	Notes
Not Budgeting for High Costs	**Create a Realistic Budget**: Research and plan for Switzerland's high cost of living. A picnic could save you 200 CHF on eating lunch in a restaurant, depending where you are.	Switzerland is known for being expensive; plan accordingly.
Not Using Public Transportation Efficiently	**Invest in Swiss Travel Pass**: Utilize the Swiss Travel Pass for unlimited travel on trains, buses, and boats.	The pass offers convenience and cost savings for transportation.
Exchanging Money at Airports	**Use Local ATMs for Better Rates**: Withdraw Swiss Francs from ATMs for competitive exchange rates.	Airport currency exchange kiosks may have less favorable rates.
Ignoring Currency Exchange Fluctuations	**Monitor Exchange Rates**: Keep an eye on exchange rates and exchange money when rates are favorable.	Be aware of currency fluctuations to maximize your budget.
Overlooking Credit Card Fees	**Use No Foreign Transaction Fee Cards**: Opt for credit cards without foreign transaction fees for purchases.	Check with your bank for fee-free options before traveling.
Eating Only in Restaurants	**Explore Local Markets and Groceries**: Save money by enjoying picnics with fresh, local products from the too good to go app.	Local markets offer delicious and cost-effective food options.
Overlooking Free Activities	**Embrace Nature and Free Attractions**: Explore Switzerland's stunning landscapes and take advantage of free activities.	Not all memorable experiences require significant spending.
Ignoring Local Transportation Options	**Take Advantage of Regional Passes**: Consider regional passes for specific areas or cities for discounted transportation.	Regional passes can be more cost-effective for short stays.
Neglecting to Book Accommodations in Advance	**Book Early and Explore Alternatives**: Secure accommodations in advance for better rates. Explore hostels, guesthouses, and Airbnb options.	Popular destinations may have limited availability during peak seasons.
Overspending on Ski Resorts	**Visit Lesser-Known Resorts**: Explore lesser-known ski resorts for more affordable options.	Popular resorts can be pricier; consider alternatives for a budget-friendly ski experience.
Not Considering Package Deals	**Explore Package Deals**: Look for bundled deals that include accommodations, transportation, and activities.	Packages can offer overall cost savings compared to individual bookings.

Checklist of top 20 things to do in Switzerland

☑ **Explore the Swiss Alps:** Take in the breathtaking landscapes, go hiking, and enjoy winter sports in iconic destinations like Zermatt and Jungfrau Region.

☑ **Visit Interlaken:** Nestled between Lake Thun and Lake Brienz, Interlaken offers stunning views and a gateway to the mountains.

☑ **Cruise on Lake Geneva:** Enjoy a boat cruise on Lake Geneva, surrounded by picturesque towns and the Alps.

☑ **Discover Lucerne:** Explore the Chapel Bridge, Water Tower, and Lion Monument in this charming city by Lake Lucerne.

☑ **Take a scenic train ride:** Experience world-famous train journeys like the Glacier Express or Bernina Express.

☑ **Explore Bern:** Visit the UNESCO-listed Old Town, the Bear Park, and the Federal Palace in Switzerland's capital.

☑ **Go Skiing in Verbier:** Experience world-class skiing in Verbier, a renowned Swiss ski resort.

☑ **Visit the Matterhorn:** Iconic mountain in Zermatt, known for its pyramid shape and challenging climbs.

☑ **Explore Zurich:** Discover the cultural richness, museums, and vibrant nightlife in Switzerland's largest city.

☑ **Cruise on Lake Lucerne:** Enjoy a boat trip on Lake Lucerne, surrounded by mountains and charming villages.

☑ **Visit Rhine Falls:** Experience the power and beauty of Europe's largest waterfall near Schaffhausen.

☑ **Discover Swiss Museums:** Explore museums like the Swiss National Museum and Kunsthaus Zurich.

☑ **Take a boat trip on Lake Zurich:** Enjoy a relaxing boat ride on Lake Zurich with views of the cityscape.

☑ **Tour Chillon Castle:** Explore the medieval Chillon Castle on the shores of Lake Geneva.

☑ **Visit Jungfraujoch:** Experience the "Top of Europe" with breathtaking views from the Jungfraujoch railway station.

☑ **Explore Montreux:** Famous for its annual Jazz Festival, Montreux offers a picturesque lakeside setting.

☑ **Hike in the Lauterbrunnen Valley:** Discover stunning waterfalls and picturesque villages in this beautiful valley.

☑ **Visit the Swiss Museum of Transport in Lucerne:** Explore the history of transportation in Switzerland.

- ✅ **Go Tobogganing in Grindelwald:** Enjoy a thrilling toboggan ride in the scenic town of Grindelwald.
- ✅ **Experience Swiss Chocolate:** Indulge in Swiss chocolate, visit a chocolate factory, or attend a chocolate-making workshop.

Historical events that will help you make sense of Switzerland

Understanding Switzerland's history is crucial to making sense of its present-day political, cultural, and social landscape. Here are some key historical events that have shaped Switzerland:

So, back in 1291, the cool cats of Uri, Schwyz, and Unterwalden got together and formed what we now call the Old Swiss Confederacy. Their alliance, sealed with the Federal Charter, is like the OG document of modern Switzerland.

Fast forward to the 16th century, and Switzerland goes through a bit of a spiritual makeover during the Swiss Reformation. Think Huldrych Zwingli in Zurich and John Calvin in Geneva – religious face-off alert!

After some Napoleonic Wars drama, the Congress of Vienna in 1814-1815 gives Switzerland a big thumbs up for perpetual neutrality. It's like Switzerland's official stamp saying, "We're staying out of the fight!"

Then comes the Sonderbund War in 1847 – a clash of Catholic and Protestant cantons. Spoiler alert: the federal government wins, and Swiss unity gets another boost.
In 1848, the Federal Constitution is adopted, marking the birth of the modern Swiss federal state. Federalism, direct democracy, and individual rights become the cool kids on the block.

Zooming into the 20th century, Switzerland pulls off the superhero move of staying neutral in both World War I and II. It's like the peacekeeper central, offering a safe space for diplomacy and humanitarian efforts.

In 1971, Swiss women join the voting party at the federal level. Some cantons had already been groovy with women's suffrage, but this was the nationwide shindig.
Then, in 2002, Switzerland takes a bold step and joins the United Nations. Goodbye to the "not being a member" era!

The 1990s and 2000s roll around, and Switzerland, though not fully on the EU guest list, decides to dance with them in the form of some nifty bilateral agreements. Economic and political cooperation – it's like Switzerland saying, "Let's be friends."

Last but not least, Switzerland's banking scene, known for its secrecy vibes, gets a bit of an international spotlight. They've been making moves to address financial transparency concerns – like a makeover for the banking world.

So there you have it – Switzerland's journey through time, complete with alliances, wars, peace vibes, and even a bit of financial drama.

The secret to saving HUGE amounts of money when travelling to Switzerland is...

Your mindset. Money is an emotional topic, if you associate words like cheapskate, Miser (and its £9.50 to go into Charles Dickens London house, oh the Irony) with being thrifty when traveling you are likely to say 'F-it' and spend your money needlessly because you associate pain with saving money. You pay now for an immediate reward. Our brains are prehistoric; they focus on surviving day to day. Travel companies and hotels know this and put trillions into making you believe you will be happier when you spend on their products or services. Our poor brains are up against outdated programming and an onslaught of advertisements bombarding us with the message: spending money on travel equals PLEASURE. To correct this carefully lodged propaganda in your frontal cortex, you need to imagine your future self.

Saving money does not make you a cheapskate. It makes you smart. How do people get rich? They invest their money. They don't go out and earn it; they let their money earn more money. So every time you want to spend money, imagine this: while you travel, your money is working for you, not you for money. While you sleep, the money, you've invested is going up and up. That's a pleasure a pricey entrance fee can't give you. Thinking about putting your money to work for you tricks your brain into believing you are not withholding pleasure from yourself, you are saving your money to invest so you can go to even more amazing places. You are thus turning thrifty travel into a pleasure fueled sport.

When you've got money invested - If you want to splash your cash on a first-class airplane seat - you can. I can't tell you how to invest your money, only that you should. Saving $20 on taxis doesn't seem like much, but over time you could save upwards of $15,000 a year, which is a deposit for a house which you can rent on Airbnb to finance more travel. Your brain making money looks like your brain on cocaine, so tell yourself saving money is making money.

Scientists have proved that imagining your future self is the easiest way to associate pleasure with saving money. You can download FaceApp — which will give you a picture of what you will look like older and grayer, or you can take a deep breath just before spending money and ask yourself if you will regret the purchase later.

The easiest ways to waste money traveling are:

Getting a taxi. The solution to this is to always download the google map before you go. Many taxi drivers will drive you around for 15 minutes when the place you were trying to get to is a 5-minute walk… remember while not getting an overpriced taxi to tell yourself, 'I am saving money to free myself for more travel.'
Spending money on overpriced food when hungry. The solution: carry snacks. A banana and an apple will cost you, in most places, less than a dollar.

Spending on entrance fees to top-rated attractions. If you really want to do it, spend the money happily. If you're conflicted, sleep on it. I don't regret spending $200 on a sky dive over the Great Barrier Reef; I regret going to the top of the shard on a cloudy day in Switzerland for $60. Only you can know, but make sure it's your decision and not the marketing directors at said top-rated attraction.

Telling yourself 'you only have the chance to see/eat/experience it now'. While this might be true, make sure YOU WANT to spend the money. Money spent is money you can't invest, and often you can have the same experience for much less.

You can experience luxurious travel on a small budget, which will trick your brain into thinking you're already a high-roller, which will mean you'll be more likely to act like one and invest your money. Stay in five-star hotels for $5 by booking on the day of your stay on booking.com to enjoy last-minute deals. You can go to fancy restaurants using daily deal sites. Ask your airline about last-minute upgrades to first-class or business. I paid $100 extra on a $179 ticket to Cuba from Germany to be bumped to Business Class. When you ask, it will surprise you what you can get both at hotels and airlines.

Travel, as the saying goes, is the only thing you spend money on that makes you richer. You can easily waste money, making it difficult to enjoy that metaphysical wealth. The biggest money saving secret is to turn bargain hunting into a pleasurable activity, not an annoyance. Budgeting consciously can be fun, don't feel disappointed because you don't spend the $60 to go into an attraction. Feel good because soon that $60 will soon earn money for you. Meaning, you'll have the time and money to enjoy more metaphysical wealth while your bank balance increases.

So there it is. You can save a thousands by being strategic with your trip planning. We've arranged everything in the guide to offer the best bang for your buck. Which means we took the view that if it's not an excellent investment for your money, we wouldn't include it. Why would a guide called 'Super Cheap' include lots of overpriced attractions? That said, if you think we've missed something or have unanswered questions, ping me an email: philgtang@gmail.com I'm on central Europe time and usually reply within 8 hours of getting your mail. We like to think of our guide books as evolving organisms helping our readers travel better cheaper. We use reader questions via email to update this book year round so you'll be helping other readers and yourself.

Don't put your dreams off!

Time is a currency you never get back and travel is its greatest return on investment. Plus, now you know you can visit Switzerland for a fraction of the price most would have you believe.

Thank you for reading

Dear **Lovely Reader**,

If you have found this book useful, please consider writing a quick review on Online Retailers.

One person from every 1000 readers leaves a review on Online Retailers. It would mean more than you could ever know if you were one of our 1 in 1000 people to take the time to write a brief review.

Thank you so much for reading again and for spending your time and investing your trips future in Super Cheap Insider Guides.

One last note, please don't listen to anyone who says 'Oh no, you can't visit Switzerland on a budget'. Unlike you, they didn't have this book. You can do ANYWHERE on a budget with the right insider advice and planning. Sure, learning to travel to Switzerland on a budget that doesn't compromise on anything or drastically compromise on safety or comfort levels is a skill, but this guide has done the detective work for you. Now it is time for you to put the advice into action.

Phil and the Super Cheap Insider Guides Team

P.S If you need any more super cheap tips we'd love to hear from you e-mail me at philgtang@gmail.com, we have a lot of contacts in every region, so if there's a specific bargain you're hunting we can help you find it.

DISCOVER YOUR NEXT VACATION

☑ **LUXURY ON A BUDGET APPROACH**
☑ **CHOOSE FROM 107 DESTINATIONS**
☑ **EACH BOOK PACKED WITH REAL-TIME LOCAL TIPS**

All are available in Paperback and e-book on Online Retailers:
https://www.Online Retailers.com/dp/B09C2DHQG5

Several are available as audiobooks. You can watch excerpts of ALL for FREE on YouTube: https://youtube.com/channel/UCxo9YV8-M9P1cFosU-Gjnqg

COUNTRY GUIDES

Super Cheap AUSTRALIA
Super Cheap CANADA
Super Cheap DENMARK
Super Cheap FINLAND
Super Cheap FRANCE
Super Cheap GERMANY
Super Cheap ICELAND
Super Cheap ITALY
Super Cheap IRELAND
Super Cheap JAPAN
Super Cheap LUXEMBOURG
Super Cheap MALDIVES 2024
Super Cheap NEW ZEALAND
Super Cheap NORWAY
Super Cheap SPAIN
Super Cheap SWITZERLAND

MORE GUIDES

Super Cheap ADELAIDE 2024
Super Cheap ALASKA 2024
Super Cheap AUSTIN 2024
Super Cheap BANGKOK 2024
Super Cheap BARCELONA 2024
Super Cheap BELFAST 2024
Super Cheap BERMUDA 2024
Super Cheap BORA BORA 2024
Super Cheap Great Barrier Reef 2024
Super Cheap CAMBRIDGE 2024
Super Cheap CANCUN 2024
Super Cheap CHIANG MAI 2024
Super Cheap CHICAGO 2024
Super Cheap DOHA 2024

Super Cheap DUBAI 2024
Super Cheap DUBLIN 2024
Super Cheap EDINBURGH 2024
Super Cheap GALWAY 2024
Super Cheap LAS VEGAS 2024
Super Cheap LIMA 2024
Super Cheap LISBON 2024
Super Cheap MALAGA 2024
Super Cheap Machu Pichu 2024
Super Cheap MIAMI 2024
Super Cheap Milan 2024
Super Cheap NASHVILLE 2024
Super Cheap NEW ORLEANS 2024
Super Cheap NEW YORK 2024
Super Cheap PARIS 2024
Super Cheap SEYCHELLES 2024
Super Cheap SINGAPORE 2024
Super Cheap ST LUCIA 2024
Super Cheap TORONTO 2024
Super Cheap TURKS AND CAICOS 2024
Super Cheap VENICE 2024
Super Cheap VIENNA 2024
Super Cheap YOSEMITE 2024
Super Cheap ZURICH 2024
Super Cheap ZANZIBAR 2024

Bonus Travel Hacks

I've included these bonus travel hacks to help you plan and enjoy your trip to Switzerland cheaply, joyfully, and smoothly. Perhaps they will even inspire you to start or renew a passion for long-term travel.

Common pitfalls when it comes to allocating money to <u>your desires</u> while traveling

Beware of Malleable mental accounting

Let's say you budgeted spending only $30 per day in Switzerland but then you say well if I was at home I'd be spending $30 on food as an everyday purchase so you add another $30 to your budget. Don't fall into that trap as the likelihood is you still have expenses at home even if its just the cost of keeping your freezer going.

Beware of impulse purchases in Switzerland

Restaurants that you haven't researched and just idle into can sometimes turn out to be great, but more often, they turn out to suck, especially if they are near tourist attractions. Make yourself a travel itinerary including where you'll eat breakfast and lunch. Dinner is always more expensive, so the meal best to enjoy at home or as a takeaway. This book is full of incredible cheap eats. All you have to do is plan to go to them.

Social media and FOMO (Fear of Missing Out)

'The pull of seeing acquaintances spend money on travel can often be a more powerful motivator to spend more while traveling than seeing an advertisement.' Beware of what you allow to influence you and go back to the question, what's the best money I can spend today?

Now-or-never sales strategies

One reason tourists are targeted by salespeople is the success of the now-or-never strategy. If you don't spend the money now… your never get the opportunity again. Rarely is this true.

Instead of spending your money on something you might not actually desire, take five minutes. Ask yourself, do I really want this? And return to the answer in five minutes. Your body will either say an absolute yes with a warm, excited feeling or a no with a weak, obscure feeling.

Unexpected costs

> **"Holding on to anger is like grasping a hot coal with the intent of throwing it at someone else; you only hurt yourself." The Buddha.**

One downside to traveling is unexpected costs. When these spring up from airlines, accommodation providers, tours and on and on, they feel like a punch in the gut. During the pandemic my earnings fell to 20% of what they are normally. No one was traveling, no one was buying travel guides. My accountant out of nowhere significantly raised his fee for the year despite the fact there was a lot less money to count. I was so angry I consulted a lawyer who told me you will spend more taking him to court than you will paying his bill. I had to get myself into a good feeling place before I paid his bill, so I googled how to feel good paying someone who has scammed you.

The answer: Write down that you will receive 10 times the amount you are paying from an unexpected source. I did that. Four months later, the accountant wrote to me. He had applied for a COVID subsidy for me and I would receive… you guessed it almost exactly 10 times his fee.

Make of that what you want. I don't wish to get embroiled in a conversation about what many term 'woo-woo', but the result of my writing that I would receive 10 times the amount made me feel much, much better when paying him. And ultimately, that was a gift in itself. So next time some airline or train operator or hotel/ Airbnb sticks you with an unexpected fee, immediately write that you will receive 10 times the amount you are paying from an unexpected source. Rise your vibe and skip the added price of feeling angry.

Hack your allocations for your Switzerland Trip

"The best trick for saving is to eliminate the decision to save." Perry Wright of Duke University.

Put the money you plan to spend in Switzerland on a pre-paid card in the local currency. This cuts out two problems - not knowing how much you've spent and totally avoiding expensive currency conversion fees.

You could even create separate spaces. This much for transportation, this for tours/entertainment, accommodation and food. We are reluctant to spend money that is pre-assigned to categories or uses.

Write that you want to enjoy a $3,000 trip for $500 to your Switzerland trip. Countless research shows when you put goals in writing, you have a higher chance of following through.

Spend all the money you want to on buying experiences in Switzerland

"Experiences are like good relatives that stay for a while and then leave. Objects are like relatives who move in and stay past their welcome." Daniel Gilbert, psychologist from Harvard University.

Economic and psychological research shows we are happier buying brief experiences on vacation rather than buying stuff to wear so give yourself freedom to spend on experiences knowing that the value you get back is many many times over.

Make saving money a game

There's one day a year where all the thrift shops where me and my family live sell everything there for a $1. My wife and I hold a contest where we take $5 and buy an entire outfit for each other. Whoever's outfit is liked more wins. We also look online to see whose outfit would have cost more to buy new. This year, my wife even snagged me an Armani coat for $1. I liked the coat when she showed it to me, but when I found out it was $500 new; I liked it and wore it a lot more.

Quadruple your money

Every-time you want to spend money, imagine it quadrupled. So the $10 you want to spend is actually $40. Now imagine that what you want to buy is four times the price. Do you still want it? If yes, go enjoy. If not, you've just saved yourself money, know you can choose to invest it in a way that quadruples or allocate it to something you really want to give you a greater return.

Understand what having unlimited amounts of money to spend in Switzerland actually looks like

Let's look at what it would be like to have unlimited amounts of money to spend on your trip to Switzerland.

Isolation

You take a private jet to your private Switzerland hotel. There you are lavished with the best food, drink, and entertainment. Spending vast amounts of money on vacation equals being isolated.

If you're on your honeymoon and you want to be alone with your Amore, this is wonderful, but it can be equally wonderful to make new friends. Know this a study 'carried out by Brigham Young University, Utah found that while obesity increased risk of death by 30%, loneliness increased it by half.'

Comfort

Money can buy you late check outs of five-star hotels and priority boarding on airlines, all of which add up to comfort. But as this book has shown you, saving money in Switzerland doesn't minimize comfort, that's just a lie travel agencies littered with glossy brochures want you to believe.

You can do late-check outs for free with the right credit cards and priority boarding can be purchased with a lot of airlines from $4. If you want to go big with first-class or business, flights offset your own travel costs by renting your own home or you can upgrade at the airport often for a fraction of what you would have paid booking a business flight online.

MORE TIPS TO FIND CHEAP FLIGHTS

"The use of travelling is to regulate imagination by reality, and instead of thinking how things may be, to see them as they are." Samuel Jackson

If you're working full-time, you can save yourself a lot of money by requesting your time off from work starting in the middle of the week. Tuesdays and Wednesdays are the cheapest days to fly. You can save thousands just by adjusting your time off.

The simplest secret to booking cheap flights is open parameters. Let's say you want to fly from Chicago to Paris. You enter the USA in from and select Switzerland under to. You may find flights from New York City to Paris for $70. Then you just need to find a cheap flight to NYC. Make sure you calculate full costs, including if you need airport accommodation and of course getting to and from airports, **but in nearly every instance open parameters will save you at least half the cost of the flight.**

 If you're not sure about where you want to go, use open parameters to show you the cheapest destinations from your city. Start with skyscanner.net they include the low-cost airlines that others like Kayak leave out. Google Flights can also show you cheap destinations. To see these leave the WHERE TO section blank. Open parameters can also show you the cheapest dates to fly. If you're flexible, you can save up to 80% of the flight cost. Always check the weather at your destination before you book. Sometimes a $400 flight will be $20, because it's monsoon season. But hey, if you like the rain, why not?

ALWAYS USE A PRIVATE BROWSER TO BOOK FLIGHTS

Skyscanner and other sites track your IP address and put prices up and down based on what they determine your strength of conviction to buy. e.g. if you've booked one-way and are looking for the return, these sites will jack the prices up by in most cases 50%. Incognito browsing pays.

Use a VPN such as Hola to book your flight from your destination

Install Hola, change your destination to the country you are flying to. The location from which a ticket is booked can affect the price significantly as algorithms consider local buying power.

Choose the right time to buy your ticket.

Choose the right time to buy your ticket, as purchasing tickets on a Sunday has been proven to be cheaper. If you can only book during the week, try to do it on a Tuesday.

Mistake fares

Email alerts from individual carriers are where you can find the best 'mistake fares". This is where a computer error has resulted in an airline offering the wrong fare. In my experience, it's best to sign up to individual carriers email lists, but if you ARE lazy Secret Flying puts together a daily roster of mistake fares. Visit https://www.secretflying.com/errorfare/ to see if there're any errors that can benefit you.

Fly late for cheaper prices

Red-eye flights, the ones that leave later in the day, are typically cheaper and less crowded, so aim to book that flight if possible. You will also get through the airport much quicker at the end of the day. Just make sure there's ground transport available for when you land. You don't want to save $50 on the airfare and spend it on a taxi to your accommodation.

Use this APP for same day flights

If your plans are flexible, use 'Get The Flight Out' (http://www.gtfoflights.com/) a fare tracker Hopper that shows you same-day deeply discounted flights. This is best for long-haul flights with major carriers. You can often find a British Airways round-trip from JFK Airport to Heathrow for $300. If you booked this in advance, you'd pay at least double.

Take an empty water bottle with you

Airport prices on food and drinks are sky high. It disgusts me to see some airports charging $10 for a bottle of water. ALWAYS take an empty water bottle with you. It's relatively unknown, but most airports have drinking water fountains past the security check. Just type in your airport name to wateratairports.com to locate the fountain. Then once you've passed security (because they don't allow you to take 100ml or more of liquids) you can freely refill your bottle with water.

Round-the-World (RTW) Tickets

It is always cheaper to book your flights using a DIY approach. First, you may decide you want to stay longer in one country, and a RTW will charge you a hefty fee for changing your flight. Secondly, it all depends on where and when you travel and as we have discussed, there are many ways to ensure you pay way less than $1,500 for a year of flights. If you're travelling long-haul, the best strategy is to buy a return ticket, say New York, to Bangkok and then take cheap flights or transport around Asia and even to Australia and beyond.

Cut your costs to and from airports

Don't you hate it when getting to and from the airport is more expensive than your flight! And this is true in so many cities, especially European ones. For some reason, Google often shows the most expensive options. Use Omio to compare the cheapest transport options and save on airport transfer costs.

Car sharing instead of taxis

Check if Switzerland has car sharing at the airport. Often they'll be tons of cars parked at the airport that are half the price of taking a taxi into the city. In most instances, you register your driving licence on an app and scan the code on the car to get going.

Checking Bags

Sometimes you need to check bags. If you do, put an AirTag inside. That way, you'll be about to see when you land where your bag is. This saves you the nail biting wait at baggage claim. And if worse comes to worst, and you see your bag is actually in another city, you can calmly stroll over to customer services and show them where your bag is.

Is it cheaper and more convenient to send your bags ahead?

Before you check your bags, check if it's cheaper to send them ahead of you with sendmybag.com obviously if you're staying in an Airbnb, you'll need to ask the hosts permission or you can time them to arrive the day after you. Hotels are normally very amenable.

What Credit Card Gives The Best Air Miles?

You can slash the cost of flights just for spending on a piece of plastic.

LET'S TALK ABOUT DEBT

Before we go into the best cards for each country, let's first talk about debt. The US system offers the best and biggest rewards. Why? Because they rely on the fact that many people living in the US will not pay their cards in full and the card will earn the bank significant interest payments. Other countries have a very different attitude towards money, debt, and saving than Americans. Thus in Germany and Austria the offerings aren't as favourable as the UK, Switzerland and Australia, where debt culture is more widely embraced. The takeaway here is this: **Only spend on one of these cards when you have set-up an automatic total monthly balance repayment. Don't let banks profit from your lizard brain!**

The best air-mile credit cards for those living in the UK

Amex Preferred Rewards Gold comes out top for those living in the UK for 2024.

Here are the benefits:

- 20,000-point bonus on £3,000 spend in first three months. These can be used towards flights with British Airways, Virgin Atlantic, Emirates and Etihad, and often other rewards, such as hotel stays and car hire.
- 1 point per £1 spent
- 1 point = 1 airline point
- Two free visits a year to airport lounges
- No fee in year one, then £140/yr

The downside:

- Fail to repay fully and it's 59.9% rep APR interest, incl fee

You'll need to cancel before the £140/yr fee kicks in year two if you want to avoid it.

The best air-mile credit cards for those living in Canada

Aeroplan is the superior rewards program in Canada. The card has a high earn rate for Aeroplan Points, generating 1.5 points per $1 spent on eligible purchases. Look at the specifics of the eligible purchases https://www.aircanada.com/ca/en/aco/home/aeroplan/earn.html. If you're not spending on these things AMEX's Membership Rewards program offers you the best returns in Canada.

The best air-mile credit cards for those living in Germany

If you have a German bank account, you can apply for a Lufthansa credit card.

Earn 50,000 award miles if you spend $3,000 in purchases and paying the annual fee, both within the first 90 days.

Earn 2 award miles per $1 spent on ticket purchases directly from Miles & More integrated airline partners.

Earn 1 award mile per $1 spent on all other purchases.

The downsides

the €89 annual fee

Limited to fly with Lufthansa and its partners but you can capitalise on perks like the companion pass and airport lounge vouchers.

You need excellent credit to get this card.

The best air-mile credit cards for those living in Austria

"In Austria, Miles & More offers you a special credit card. You get miles for each purchase with the credit card. The Miles & More program calculates miles earned based on the distance flown and booking class. For European flights, the booking class is a flat rate. For intercontinental flights, mileage is calculated by multiplying the booking class by the distance flown." They offer a calculator so you can see how many points you could earn: https://www.miles-and-more.com/at/en/earn/airlines/mileage-calculator.html

The best air-mile credit cards for those living in Switzerland:

"The American Express card is the best known and oldest to earn miles, thanks to its membership Rewards program. When making payments with this card, points are added, which can then be exchanged for miles from airlines such as Iberia, Air Europa, Emirates or Alitalia." More information is available here: https://www.americanexpress.com/es-es/

The best air-mile credit cards for those living in Australia

ANZ Rewards Black comes out top for 2024.

180,000 bonus ANZ Reward Points (can get an $800 gift card) and $0 annual fee for the first year with the ANZ Rewards Black
Points Per Spend: 1 Velocity point on purchases of up to $5,000 per statement period and 0.5 Velocity points thereafter.
Annual Fee: $0 in the first year, then $375 after.
Ns no set minimum income required, however, there is a minimum credit limit of $15,000 on this card.

Here are some ways you can hack points onto this card: https://www.pointhacks.com.au/credit-cards/anz-rewards-black-guide/

The best air-mile credit card solution for those living in the USA with a POOR credit score

The downside to Airline Mile cards is that they require good or excellent credit scores, meaning 690 or higher.

If you have bad credit and want to use credit card air lines you will need to rebuild your credit poor. The Credit One Bank® Platinum Visa® for Rebuilding Credit is a good credit card for people with bad credit who don't want to place a deposit on a secured card. The Credit One Platinum Visa offers a $300 credit limit, rewards, and the potential for credit-limit increases, which in time will help rebuild your score.

PLEASE don't sign-up for any of these cards if you can't trust yourself to repay it in full monthly. This will only lead to stress for you.

Frequent Flyer Memberships

"Points" and "miles" are often used interchangeably, but they're usually two very different things. Maximise and diversify your rewards by utilising both.

A frequent-flyer program (FFP) is a loyalty program offered by an airline. They are designed to encourage airline customers to fly more to accumulate points (also called miles, kilometres, or segments) which can be redeemed for air travel or other rewards.

You can sign up with any FFP program for free. There are three major airline alliances in the world: Oneworld, SkyTeam and Star Alliance. I am with One World https://www.oneworld.com/members because the points can be accrued and used for most flights.

The best return on your points is to use them for international business or first class flights with lie-flat seats. You would need 3 times more miles compared to an economy flight, but if you paid cash, you'd pay 5 - 10 times more than the cost of the economy flight, so it really pays to use your points only for upgrades. The worst value for your miles is to buy an economy seat or worse, a gift from the airlines gift-shop.

Sign up for a family/household account to pool miles together. If you share a common address, you can claim the miles with most airlines. You can use AwardWallet to keep track of your miles. Remember that they only last for 2 years, so use them before they expire.

How to get 70% off a Cruise

An average cruise can set you back $4,000. If you dream of cruising the oceans, but find the pricing too high, look at repositioning cruises. You can save as much as 70% by taking a cruise which takes the boat back to its home port.

These one-way itineraries take place during low cruise seasons when ships have to reposition themselves to locations where there's warmer weather.

To find a repositioning cruise, go to vacationstogo.com/repositioning_cruises.cfm. This simple and often overlooked booking trick is great for avoiding long flights with children and can save you so much money!

It's worth noting we don't have any affiliations with any travel service or provider. The links we suggest are chosen based on our experience of finding the best deals.

Relaxing at the Airport

The best way to relax at the airport is in a lounge where they provide free food, drinks, comfortable chairs, luxurious amenities (many have showers) and, if you're lucky, a peaceful ambience. If you're there for a longer time, look for Airport Cubicles, sleep pods which charge by the hour.

You can use your FFP Card (Frequent Flyer Memberships) to get into select lounges for free. Check your eligibility before you pay.

If you're travelling a lot, I'd recommend investing in a Priority Pass for the airport.

It includes 850-plus airport lounges around the world. The cost is $99 for the year and $27 per lounge visit or you can pay $399 for the year all inclusive.

If you need a lounge for a one-off day, you can get a Day Pass. Buy it online for a discount, it always works out cheaper than buying at the airport. Use www.LoungePass.com.

Lounges are also great if you're travelling with kids, as they're normally free for kids and will definitely cost you less than snacks for your little ones. The rule is that kids should be seen and not heard, so consider this before taking an overly excited child who wants to run around, or you might be asked to leave even after you've paid.

How to spend money

Bank ATM fees vary from $2.50 per transaction to as high as $5 or more, depending on the ATM and the country. You can completely skip those fees by paying with card and using a card which can hold multiple currencies.

Budget travel hacking begins with a strategy to spend without fees. Your individual strategy depends on the country you legally reside in as to what cards are available. Happily there are some fin-tech solutions which can save you thousands on those pesky ATM withdrawal fees and are widely available globally. Here are a selection of cards you can pre-charge with currency for Switzerland:

N26

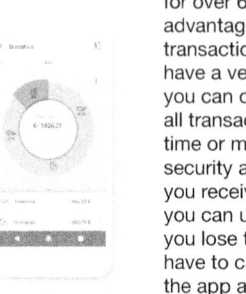

N26 is a 12-year-old digital bank. I have been using them for over 6 years. The key advantage is fee-free card transactions abroad. They have a very elegant app, where you can check your timeline for all transactions listed in real time or manage your in-app security anywhere. The card you receive is a Mastercard so you can use it everywhere. If you lose the card, you don't have to call anyone, just open the app and swipe 'lock card'. It puts your purchases into a graph automatically so you can see what you spend on. You can open an account from abroad entirely online, all you need is your passport and a camera n26.com

Revolut

Revolut is a multi-currency account that allows you to hold and exchange 29 currencies and spend fee-free abroad. It's a UK based neobank, but accepts customers from all over the world.

Wise debit card

If you're going to be in one place for a long time, the Wise debit card is like having your travel money on a card – it lets you spend money at the real exchange rate.

Monzo

Monzo is good if your UK based. They offer a fee-free UK account. Fee-free international money transfers and fee-free spending abroad.

The downside

The cards above are debit cards, meaning you need to have money in those accounts to spend it. This comes with one big downside: safety. Credit card issuers' have "zero liability" meaning you're not liable for unauthorised charges. All the cards listed above do provide cover for unauthorised charges but times vary greatly in how quickly you'd get your money back if it were stolen.

The best option is to check in your country to see which credit cards are the best for travelling and set up monthly payments to repay the whole amount so you don't pay unnecessary interest. In the USA, Schwab regularly ranks at the top for travel credit cards. Credit cards are always the safer option when abroad simply because you get your money back faster if its stolen and if you're renting cars, most will give you free insurance when you book the car rental using the card, saving you money.

Always withdraw money; never exchange.

Money exchanges, whether they be on the streets or in the airports will NEVER give you a good exchange rate. Do not bring bundles of cash. Instead, withdraw local currency from the ATM as needed and try to use only free ATMs. Many in airports charge you a fee to withdraw cash. Look for bigger ATMs attached to banks to avoid this.

Recap

- Take cash from local, non-charging ATMs for the best rates.
- Never change at airport exchange desks unless you absolutely have to, then just change just enough to be able get to a bank ATM.
- Bring a spare credit card for emergencies.
- Split cash in various places on your person (pockets, shoes) and in your luggage. It's never sensible to keep your cash or cards all in one place.
- In higher risk areas, use a money belt under your clothes or put $50 in your shoe or bra.

Revolut
Revolut is a multi-currency account that allows you to hold and exchange 29 currencies and spend fee-free abroad. It's a UK based neobank, but accepts customers from all over the world.

Wise debit card
If you're going to be in one place for a long time the Wise debit card is like having your travel money on a card – it lets you spend money at the real exchange rate.

Monzo
Monzo is good if your UK based. They offer a fee-free UK account. Fee-free international money transfers and fee-free spending abroad.

The downside

The cards above are debit cards, meaning you need to have money in those accounts to spend it. This comes with one big downside: safety. Credit card issuers' have "zero liability" meaning you're not liable for unauthorised charges. All of the cards listed above do provide cover for unauthorised charges but times vary greatly in how quickly you'd get your money back if it were stolen.

The best option is to check in your country to see which credit cards are the best for travelling and set up monthly payments to repay the whole amount so you don't pay unnecessary interest. In the USA, Schwab[4] regularly ranks at the top for travel credit cards. Credit cards are always the safer option when abroad simply because you get your money back faster if its stolen and if you're renting cars, most will give you free insurance when you book the car rental using the card, saving you money.

Always withdraw money; never exchange.

Money exchanges whether they be on the streets or in the airports will NEVER give you a good exchange rate. Do not bring bundles of cash. Instead withdraw local currency from the ATM as needed and try to use only free ATM's. Many in airports charge you a fee to withdraw cash. Look for bigger ATM's attached to banks to avoid this.

Recap

- Take cash from local, non-charging ATMs for the best rates.
- Never change at airport exchange desks unless you absolutely have to, then just change just enough to be able get to a bank ATM.
- Bring a spare credit card for emergencies.
- Split cash in various places on your person (pockets, shoes) and in your luggage. Its never sensible to keep your cash or cards all in one place.
- In higher risk areas, use a money belt under your clothes or put $50 in your shoe or bra.

---

[4] Charles Schwab High Yield Checking accounts refund every single ATM fee worldwide, require no minimum balance and have no monthly fee.

How NOT to be ripped off

"One of the great things about travel is that you find out how many good, kind people there are."
— Edith Wharton

The quote above may seem ill placed in a chapter entitled how not to be ripped off, but I included it to remind you that the vast majority of people do not want to rip you off. In fact, scammers are normally limited to three situations:

1. Around heavily visited attractions - these places are targeted purposively due to sheer footfall. Many criminals believe ripping people off is simply a numbers game.
2. In cities or countries with low-salaries or communist ideologies. If they can't make money in the country, they seek to scam foreigners. If you have travelled to India, Morocco or Cuba you will have observed this phenomenon.
3. When you are stuck and the person helping you know you have limited options.

Scammers know that most people will avoid confrontation. Don't feel bad about utterly ignoring someone and saying no. Here are six strategies to avoid being ripped off:

1. **Never ever agree to pay as much as you want. Always decide on a price before.**

Whoever you're dealing with is trained to tell you, they are uninterested in money. This is a trap. If you let people do this they will ask for MUCH MORE money at the end, and because you have used there service, you will feel obliged to pay. This is a conman's trick and nothing more.

2. Pack light

You can move faster and easier. If you take heavy luggage, you will end up taking taxis which are comparatively very costly over time.

3. NEVER use the airport taxi service. Plan to use public transport before you reach the airport.

4. Don't buy a sim card from the airport. Buy from the local supermarkets it will cost 50% less.

5. Eat at local restaurants serving regional food

Food defines culture. Exploring all delights available to the palate doesn't need to cost enormous sums.

6. **Ask the locals what something should cost,** and try not to pay over that.

7. **If you find yourself with limited options.** e.g. your taxi dumps you on the side of the road because you refuse to pay more (common in India and parts of South America) don't act desperate and negotiate as if you have other options or you will be extorted.

8. Don't blindly rely on social media[5]

Let's say you post in a Facebook group that you want tips for travelling to The Maldives. A lot of the comments you will receive come from guides, hosts and restaurants doing their own promotion. It's estimated that 50% or more of Facebook's current monthly active users are fake. And what's worse, a recent study found Social media platforms leave 95% of reported fake accounts up. These accounts are the digital versions of the men who hang around the Grand Palace in Bangkok telling tourists its closed, to divert you to shops where they will receive a commission for bringing you.

It can also be the case that genuine comments come from people who have totally different interests, beliefs and yes, budgets to yours. Make your experience your own and don't believe every comment you read.

Bottom line: use caution when accepting recommendations on social media and always fact-check with your own research.

Small tweaks on the road add up to big differences in your bank balance

Take advantage of other hotel amenities

If you fancy a swim but you're nowhere near the ocean, try the nearest hotel with a pool. As long as you buy a drink, the hotel staff will probably grant you access.

Fill up your mini bar for free.

Fill up your mini bar for free by storing things from the breakfast bar or grocery shop in your mini bar to give you a greater selection of drinks and food without the hefty price tag.

Save yourself some ironing

Use the steam from the shower to get rid of wrinkles in clothing. If something is creased, leave it trapped with the steam in the bathroom overnight for even better results.

See somewhere else for free

Opt for long stopovers, allowing you to experience another city without spending much money.

Wear your heaviest clothes

On the plane to save weight in your pack, allowing you to bring more with you. Big coats can then be used as pillows to make your flight more comfortable.

Don't get lost while you're away.

Find where you want to go using Google Maps, then type 'OK Maps' into the search bar to store this information for offline viewing.

---

[5] https://arstechnica.com/tech-policy/2019/12/social-media-platforms-leave-95-of-reported-fake-accounts-up-study-finds/

Use car renting services

Share Now or Car2Go allow you to hire a car for 2 hours for $25 in a lot of European countries.

Share Rides

Use sites like blablacar.com to find others who are driving in your direction. It can be 80% cheaper than normal transport. Just check the drivers reviews.

Use free gym passes

Get a free gym day pass by googling the name of a local gym and free day pass.

When asked by people providing you a service where you are from..

If there's no price list for the service you are asking for, when asked where you are from, Say you are from a lesser-known poorer country. I normally say Macedonia, and if they don't know where it is, add it's a poor country. If you say UK, USA, the majority of Europe bar the well-known poorer countries taxi drivers, tour operators etc will match the price to what they think you pay at home.

Set-up a New Uber/ other car hailing app account for discounts

By googling you can find offers with $50 free for new users in most cities for Uber/ Lyft/ Bolt and alike. Just set up a new gmail.com email account to take advantage.

Where and How to Make Friends

"People don't take trips, trips take people." – John Steinbeck

Become popular at the airport

Want to become popular at the airport? Pack a power bar with multiple outlets and just see how many friends you can make. It's amazing how many people forget their chargers, or who packed them in the luggage that they checked in.

Stay in Hostels

First of all, Hostels don't have to be shared dorms, and they cater to a much wider demographic than is assumed. Hostels are a better environment for meeting people than hotels, and more importantly, they tended to open up excursion opportunities that further opened up that opportunity.

Or take up a hobby

If hostels are a definite no-no for you; find an interest. Take up a hobby where you will meet people. I've dived for years and the nature of diving is you're always paired up with a dive buddy. I met a lot of interesting people that way.

Small tweaks on the road add up to big differences in your bank balance

Take advantage of other hotel's amenities

If you fancy a swim but you're nowhere near the ocean, try the nearest hotel with a pool. As long as you buy a drink, the hotel staff will likely grant you access.

Fill up your mini bar for free.

Fill up your mini bar for free by storing things from the breakfast bar or grocery shop in your mini bar to give you a greater selection of drinks and food without the hefty price tag.

Save yourself some ironing

Use the steam from the shower to get rid of wrinkles in clothing. If something is creased, leave it trapped with the steam in the bathroom overnight for even better results.

See somewhere else for free

Opt for long stopovers, allowing you to experience another city without spending much money.

Wear your heaviest clothes

on the plane to save weight in your pack, allowing you to bring more with you. Big coats can then be used as pillows to make your flight more comfortable.

Don't get lost while you're away.

Find where you want to go using Google Maps, then type 'OK Maps' into the search bar to store this information for offline viewing.

Use car renting services

Share Now or Car2Go allow you to hire a car for 2 hours for $25 in a lot of Europe.

Share Rides

Use sites like blablacar.com to find others who are driving in your direction. It can be 80% cheaper than normal transport. Just check the drivers reviews.

Use free gym passes

Get a free gym day pass by googling the name of a local gym and free day pass.

When asked by people providing you a service where you are from..

If there's no price list for the service you are asking for, when asked where you are from, Say you are from a lesser-known poorer country. I normally say Macedonia, and if they don't know where it is, add it's a poor country. If you say UK, USA, the majority of Europe bar the well-known poorer countries taxi drivers, tour operators etc will match the price to what they think you pay at home.

Set-up a New Uber/ other car hailing app account for discounts

By googling you can find offers with $50 free for new users in most cities for Uber/ Lyft/ Bolt and alike. Just set up a new gmail.com email account to take advantage.

Where and How to Make Friends

"People don't take trips, trips take people." – John Steinbeck

Become popular at the airport

Want to become popular at the airport? Pack a power bar with multiple outlets and just see how many friends you can make. It's amazing how many people forget their chargers, or who packed them in the luggage that they checked in.

Stay in Hostels

First of all, Hostels don't have to be shared dorms, and they cater to a much wider demographic than is assumed. Hostels are a better environment for meeting people than hotels, and more importantly they tended to open up excursion opportunities that further opened up that opportunity.

Or take up a hobby

If hostels are a definite no-no for you; find an interest. Take up a hobby where you will meet people. I've dived for years and the nature of diving is you're always paired up with a dive buddy. I met a lot of interesting people that way.

When unpleasantries come your way...

We all have our good and bad days travelling, and on a bad day you can feel like just taking a flight home. Here are some ways to overcome common travel problems:

Anxiety when flying

It has been over 40 years since a plane has been brought down by turbulence. Repeat that number to yourself: 40 years! Planes are built to withstand lighting strikes, extreme storms and ultimately can adjust course to get out of their way. Landing and take-off are when the most accidents happen, but you have statistically three times the chance of winning a huge jackpot lottery, then you do of dying in a plane crash.

If you feel afraid on the flight, focus on your breathing saying the word 'smooth' over and over until the flight is smooth. Always check the airline safety record on airlinerating.com I was surprised to learn Ryanair and Easyjet as much less safe than Wizz Air according to those ratings because they sell similarly priced flights. If there is extreme turbulence, I feel much better knowing I'm in a 7 star safety plane.

Wanting to sleep instead of seeing new places

This is a common problem. Just relax, there's little point doing fun things when you feel tired. Factor in jet-lag to your travel plans. When you're rested and alert you'll enjoy your new temporary home much more. Many people hate the first week of a long-trip because of jet-lag and often blame this on their first destination, but its rarely true. Ask travellers who 'hate' a particular place and you will see that very often they either had jet-lag or an unpleasant journey there.

Going over budget

Come back from a trip to a monster credit card bill? Hopefully, this guide has prevented you from returning to an unwanted bill. Of course, there are costs that can creep up and this is a reminder about how to prevent them making their way on to your credit card bill:

- To and from the airport. Solution: leave adequate time and take the cheapest method - book before.

- Baggage. Solution: take hand luggage and post things you might need to yourself.

- Eating out. Solution: go to cheap eats places and suggest those to friends.

- Parking. Solution: use apps to find free parking

- Tipping. Solution Leave a modest tip and tell the server you will write them a nice review.

- Souvenirs. Solution: fridge magnets only.

- Giving to the poor. (This one still gets me, but if you're giving away $10 a day - it adds up) Solution: volunteer your time instead and recognise that in tourist destinations many beggars are run by organised crime gangs.

Price v Comfort

I love traveling. I don't love struggling. I like decent accommodation, being able to eat properly and see places and enjoy. I am never in the mood for low-cost airlines or crappy transfers, so here's what I do to save money.

- Avoid organised tours unless you are going to a place where safety is a real issue. They are expensive and constrain your wanderlust to typical things. I only recommend them in Algeria, Iran and Papua New Guinea - where language and gender views pose serious problems all cured by a reputable tour organiser.
- Eat what the locals do.
- Cook in your Airbnb/ hostel where restaurants are expensive.
- Shop at local markets.
- Spend time choosing your flight, and check the operator on arilineratings.com
- Mix up hostels and Airbnbs. Hostels for meeting people, Airbnb for relaxing and feeling 'at home'.

Not knowing where free toilets are

Use Toilet Finder - https://play.google.com/store/apps/details?id=com.bto.toilet&hl=en

Your Airbnb is awful

Airbnb customer service is notoriously bad. Help yourself out. Try to sort things out with the host, but if you can't, take photos of everything e.g bed, bathroom, mess, doors, contact them within 24 hours. Tell them you had to leave and pay for new accommodation. Ask politely for a full refund including booking fees. With photographic evidence and your new accommodation receipt, they can't refuse.

The airline loses your bag

Go to the Luggage desk before leaving the airport and report the bag missing. Hopefully you've headed the advice to put an AirTag in your checked bag and you can show them where to find your bag. Most airlines will give you an overnight bag, ask where you're staying and return the bag to you within three days. It's extremely rare for Airlines to lose your bag due to technological innovation, but if that happens you should submit an insurance claim after the three days is up, including receipts for everything you had to buy in the interim.

Your travel companion lets you down

Whether it's a breakup or a friend cancelling, it sucks and can ramp up costs. The easiest solution to finding a new travel companion is to go to a well-reviewed hostel and find someone you want to travel with. You should spend at least three days getting to know this person before you suggest travelling together. Finding someone in person is always better than finding someone online, because you can get a better idea of whether you will have a smooth journey together. Travel can make or break friendships.

Culture shock

I had one of the strongest culture shocks while spending 6 months in Japan. It was overwhelming how much I had to prepare when I went outside of the door (googling words and sentences what to use, where to go, which station and train line to use, what is this food called in Japanese and how does its look etc.). I was so tired constantly but in the end I just let go and went with my extremely bad Japanese. If you feel culture shocked its because your brain is referencing your surroundings to what you know. Stop comparing, have Google translate downloaded and relax.

Your Car rental insurance is crazy expensive

I always use carrentals.com and book with a credit card. Most credit cards will give you free insurance for the car, so you don't need to pay the extra. Some unsavoury companies will bump the price up when you arrive. Ask to speak to a manager. If this doesn't resolve, it google "consumer ombudsman for NAME OF COUNTRY." and seek an immediate full refund on the balance difference you paid. It is illegal in most countries to alter the price of a rental car when the person arrives to pickup a pre-arranged car.

A note on Car Rental Insurance

Always always always rent a car with a credit card that has rental vehicle coverage built into the card and is automatically applied when you rent a car. Then there's no need to buy additional rental insurance (check with your card on the coverage they protect some exclude collision coverage). Do yourself a favour when you step up to the desk to rent the car tell the agent you're already covered and won't be buying anything today. They work on commission and you'll save time and your patience avoiding the upselling.

You're sick

First off ALWAYS, purchase travel insurance. Including emergency transport up to $500k even to back home, which is usually less than $10 additional. I use https://www.comparethemarket.com/travel-insurance/ to find the best days. If I am sick I normally check into a hotel with room service and ride it out.

Make a Medication Travel Kit

Take travel sized medications with you:

- Antidiarrheal medication (for example, bismuth subsalicylate, loperamide)

- Medicine for pain or fever (such as acetaminophen, aspirin, or ibuprofen)

- Throat Lozenges

Save yourself from most travel related hassles

- Do not make jokes with immigration and customs staff. A misunderstanding can lead to HUGE fines.

- Book the most direct flight you can find nonstop if possible.

- Carry a US$50 bill for emergency cash. I have entered a country and all ATM and credit card systems were down. US$ can be exchanged nearly anywhere in the world and is useful in extreme situations, but where possible don't exchange, as you will lose money.

- Check, and recheck, required visas and such BEFORE the day of your trip. Some countries, for instance, require a ticket out of the country in order to enter. Others, like the US and Australia, require electronic authorisation in advance.

- Airport security is asinine and inconsistent around the world. Keep this in mind when connecting flights. Always leave at least 2 hours for international connections or international to domestic. In Stansted for example, they force you to buy one of their plastic bags, and remove your liquids from your own plastic bag…. just to make money from you. And this adds to the time it will take to get through security, so lines are long.

- Wiki travel is perfect to use for a lay of the land.

- Expensive luggage rarely lasts longer than cheap luggage, in my experience. Fancy leather bags are toast with air travel.

Food

- When it comes to food, eat in local restaurants, not tourist-geared joints. Any place with the menu in three or more languages is going to be overpriced.

- Take a spork - a knife, spoon and fork all in one.

Water Bottle

Take a water bottle with a filter. We love these ones from Water to Go.

Empty it before airport security and separate the bottle and filter as some airport people will try and claim it has liquids…

Bug Sprays

If you're heading somewhere tropical spray your clothes with Permethrin before you travel. It lasts 40 washes and saves space in your bag. A 'Bite Away' zapper can be used after the bite to totally erase it. It cuts down on the itching and erases the bite from your skin.

Order free mini's

Don't buy those expensive travel sized toiletries, order travel sized freebies online. This gives you the opportunity to try brands you've never used before, and who knows, you might even find your new favourite soap.

Take a waterproof bag

If you're travelling alone you can swim without worrying about your phone, wallet and passport laying on the beach.

You can also use it as a source of entertainment on those ultra budget flights.

Make a private entertainment centre anywhere

Always take an eye-mask, earplugs, a scarf and a kindle reader - so you can sleep and entertain yourself anywhere!

The best Travel Gadgets

The door alarm

If you're nervous and staying in private rooms or airbnbs take a door alarm. For those times when you just don't feel safe, it can help you fall asleep. You can get tiny ones for less than $10 from Online Retailers: https://www.Online Retailers.com/Travel-door-alarm/s?k=Travel+door+alarm

Smart Blanket

Online Retailers sells a 6 in 1 heating blanket that is very useful for cold plane or bus trips. Its great if you have poor circulation as it becomes a detachable Foot Warmer: Online Retailers http://amzn.to/2hTYIOP I paid $49.00.

The coat that becomes a tent

https://www.adiff.com/products/tent-jacket. This is great if you're going to be doing a lot of camping.

Clever Tank Top with Secret Pockets

Keep your valuables safe in this top. Perfect for all climates.

on Online Retailers for $39.90

Optical Camera Lens for Smartphones and Tablets

Leave your bulky camera at home. Turn your device into a high-performance camera. Buy on Online Retailers for $9.95

Travel-sized Wireless Router with USB Media Storage

Convert any wired network to a wireless network. Buy on Online Retailers for $17.99

Buy a Scrubba Bag to wash your clothes on the go

Or a cheaper imitable. You can wash your clothes on the go.

Hacks for Families

Rent an Airbnb apartment so you can cook

Apartments are much better for families, as you have all the amenities you'd have at home. They are normally cheaper per person too. We are the first travel guide publisher to include Airbnb's in our recommendations if you think any of these need updating you can email me at philgtang@gmail.com

Shop at local markets

Eat seasonal products and local products. Get closer to the local market and observe the prices and the offer. What you can find more easily, will be the cheapest.

Take Free Tours

Download free podcast tours of the destination you are visiting. The podcast will tell you where to start, where to go, and what to look for. Often you can find multiple podcast tours of the same place. Listen to all of them if you like, each one will tell you a little something new.

Pack Extra Ear Phones

If you go on a museum tour, they often have audio guides. Instead of having to rent one for each person, take some extra earphones. Most audio tour devices have a place to plug in a second set.

Buy Souvenirs Ahead of Time

If you are buying souvenirs somewhere touristy, you are paying a premium price. By ordering the same exact products online, you can save a lot of money.

Use Cheap Transportation

Do as the locals do, including weekly passes.

Carry Reusable Water Bottles

Spending money on water and other beverages can quickly add up. Instead of paying for drinks, take some refillable water bottles.

Combine Attractions

Many major cities offer ticket bundles where one price gets you into 5 or 6 popular attractions. You will need to plan ahead of time to decide what things you plan to do on vacation and see if they are selling these activities together.

Pack Snacks

Granola bars, apples, baby carrots, bananas, cheese crackers, juice boxes, pretzels, fruit snacks, apple sauce, grapes, and veggie chips.

Stick to Carry-On Bags

Do not pay to check a large bag. Even a small child can pull a carry-on.

Visit free art galleries and museums

Just google the name + free days.

Eat Street Food

There's a lot of unnecessary fear around this. You can watch the food prepared. Go for the stands that have a steady queue.

Travel Gadgets for Families

Dropcam

Are what-if scenarios playing out in your head? Then you need Dropcam.

'Dropcam HD Internet Wi-Fi Video Monitoring Cameras help you watch what you love from anywhere. In less than a minute, you'll have it setup and securely streaming video to you over your home Wi-Fi. Watch what you love while away with Dropcam HD.'

Approximate Price: $139

Kelty-Child-Carrier

Voted as one of the best hiking essentials if you're traveling with kids and can carry a child up to 18kg.

Jetkids Bedbox

No more giving up your own personal space on the plane with this suitcase that becomes a bed.

How I got hooked on luxury on a budget travelling

'We're on holiday' is what my dad used to say to justify getting us in so much debt we lost our home and all our things when I was 11. We moved from the suburban bliss of Hemel Hempstead to a run down council estate in inner-city London, near my dad's new job as a refuge collector, a fancy word for dustbin man. I lost all my school friends while watching my dad go through a nervous breakdown.

My dad loved walking up a hotel lobby desk without a care in the world. So much so, that he booked overpriced holidays on credit cards. A lot of holidays. As it turned out, we couldn't afford any of them. In the end, my dad had no choice but to declare bankruptcy. When my mum realised, he'd racked up so much debt our family unit dissolved. A neat and perhaps as painless a summary of events that lead me to my life's passion: budget travel that doesn't compromise on fun, safety or comfort.

I started travelling full-time at the age of 18. I wrote the first Super Cheap Insider guide for friends visiting Norway - which I did for a month on less than $250. When sales reached 10,000 I decided to form the Super Cheap Insider Guides company. As I know from first-hand experience debt can be a noose around our necks, and saying 'oh come on, we're on vacation' isn't a get out of jail free card. In fact, its the reverse of what travel is supposed to bring you - freedom.

Before I embarked upon writing Super Cheap Insider guides, many, many people told me that my dream was impossible. Travelling on a budget could never be comfortable. I hope this guide has proved to you what I have known for a long-time: budget travel can feel luxurious when you know and use the insider hacks.

And apologies if I depressed you with my tale of woe. My dad is now happily remarried and works as a chef in Switzerland at a fancy hotel - the kind he used to take us to!

A final word...

There's a simple system you can use to think about budget travel. In life, we can choose two of the following: cheap, fast, or quality. So if you want it Cheap and fast you will get a lower quality service. Fast-food is the perfect example. The system holds true for purchasing anything while travelling. I always choose cheap and quality, except at times where I am really limited on time. Normally, you can make small tweaks to make this work for you. Ultimately, you must make choices about what's most important to you and heed your heart's desires.

'Your heart is the most powerful muscle in your body. Do what it says.' Jen Sincero

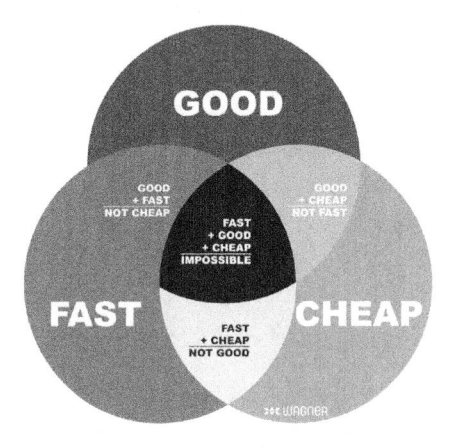

If you've found this book useful, please select some stars, it would mean genuinely make my day to see I've helped you.

Copyright

Published in Great Britain in 2024 by Super Cheap Insider Guides LTD.

Copyright © 2024 Super Cheap Insider Guides LTD.

The right of Phil G A Tang to be identified as the Author of the Work has been asserted in accordance with the Copyright, Designs and Patents Act 1988.

All rights reserved.

No part of this publication may be reproduced, stored in a retrieval system, or transmitted, in any form or by any means without the prior written permission of the publisher, nor be otherwise circulated in any form of binding or cover other than that in which it is published and without a similar condition being imposed on the subsequent purchaser.

All rights reserved. No part of this publication may be reproduced, distributed, or transmitted in any form or by any means, including photocopying, recording, or other electronic or mechanical methods, without the prior written permission of the publisher, except in the case of brief quotations embodied in critical reviews and certain other noncommercial uses permitted by copyright law.

Printed in Great Britain
by Amazon